THE PROVING
GROUND

Nine Tests That Prove Your Personal Potential

KEVIN GERALD

THE PROVING GROUND

The Proving Ground by Kevin Gerald
Published by Kevin Gerald Communications
1819 E. 72nd Street, Tacoma, WA 98404

Unless otherwise noted, Scripture quotations are from the Holy Bible, New International Version, copyright © 1973, 1978, 1984 by International Bible Society, Passages marked KJV are from the King James Version.

ISBN: 978-0-692-16021-3
Library of Congress catalog card number: 2003102783

Printed in the United States of America

Recognizing A Test

If you have ever watched cable television, you would probably recognize when the colorful pattern appears on the TV set, accompanied by chilling, high-pitched sounds. Then, a muffled announcer verifies that, "This has been a test of the Emergency Broadcast System. I repeat, this is only a test."

Wouldn't it be helpful if the trials in our lives were preceded by the announcement, "This is only a test, brought to you by the Heavenly Development System?" The challenge of life's tests is that they often catch us off guard. Even if we are alert, the test will come in disguise so that we don't recognize it. This lack of recognition is one reason many people don't pass the test, but until you pass the test, you will continue to face the test. This book will provide insight to help you better recognize and identify the times of testing in your life. There will never be an announcement, but if we increase our awareness, we can remind ourselves and others that "this is only a test."

Proving Your Personal Potential

When you get ready to buy a new car, one of the things you want to do as a wise investor is to go on a test drive in order to find out if the car is safe and right for you. Likewise, the food that we eat gets tested. Appliances are given a label

Our personal potential is unknown **until it is proven.**

with a certification number on them that verifies that they have been tested. Even airplanes go through an extensive testing process before you get in them, which I am thankful for when I am 30,000 feet in the air.

The purpose of testing is to prove the product. So, the milk we drink, the automobiles we drive, the airplanes we fly in, and many other products that we use, are all tested to prove their safety and reliability. The product has to withstand the tests way before it gets into our hands.

In that same way, human beings go through tests that determine who we are, what kind of character we have, what we can endure, how dependable and reliable we are, what causes us to lose it, and so forth. Who you are and what you are made of—your personal potential—is proven by this testing process.

I could tell myself right now that I can ride a bike backwards with no hands, but saying that doesn't prove that I can do it. I have to test my ability. You may be reading this right now thinking of areas that you feel that you still have room to prove yourself in, and that's a good thing! I like to say keep the growing going. The minute you stop growing is the minute you deny your true potential, because our personal potential is unknown until it is proven. That's right: unknown. You have abilities and opportunities that are inside of you that can be opened up, and God wants to open up, through testing. In an effort to prepare you for this time of testing, I am going to share the nine most common tests that a person experiences. Let's take a brief look at the tests that we will be looking at in the coming chapters.

1 The Test of Small Things

This test comes to prove your potential for bigger opportunities by seeing how you handle smaller ones.

2 The Motivation Test

You could be doing the right thing for the wrong reasons, so this test challenges the why behind what you do.

3 The Credibility Test

This test will prove that you maintain integrity, refusing to compromise ethics and morals in pressured circumstances.

4 The Wilderness Test

When you're in a drought or dry season, this test will prove your potential to make the changes necessary to enter the next level of maturity and prosperity in your life.

5 The Authority Test

This test comes to prove your attitude towards the authority that God has put in your life.

6 The Warfare Test

When you are in the will of God and are experiencing problems, this test will prove how you respond to adversity.

7 The Offense Test

This test will prove whether or not you are not easily offended and if you have the potential to readily forgive others.

8 The Test of Time

If things don't happen in the timing that you planned, this test comes to prove your endurance, patience, and ongoing confidence in various seasons of life.

9 The Lordship Test

This test will put you in a position or a situation where it is not easy to obey God. It is designed to prove that you will obey God's Word and God's will, even when it is not the easy thing to do.

The Difference Between Temptation And Testing

. . . .

Some people picture God dreaming up all kinds of schemes to tempt human beings, and then they picture Him sitting back in His comfortable recliner throne, watching, and saying things like, "Bet you don't make this one! Let's see if you can handle that one!" As if, being God, He gets some kind of high out of watching us being stretched, pushed, tried, and tested. That is a wrong concept of God. That is not why we have tests in life.

Here's what the Bible says in response to those thoughts:

No one should say, "God is tempting me." For God cannot be tempted by evil nor does He tempt anyone. But, each one is tempted when by his own evil desire, he is dragged away and enticed. After desire has conceived, it gives birth to sin, and sin when it is full-grown, gives birth to death. Do not be deceived. Every good and perfect gift is from above. It comes down from the Father of the heavenly lights, who does not change like shifting shadows.

James 1:13–17, NIV

So, God cannot be tempted by evil, nor does God tempt any man with evil. There is a difference between temptation and testing. I want to help you understand where temptation comes from and where testing comes from. When we really grasp hold of this subject, it will help us through the tests of life, which we will inevitably encounter.

Let me say again, a test is different than a temptation. For example, when you learn something in school, the test comes to prove what you have learned and is very valuable. A temptation, on the other hand, is not primarily intended to prove what you have learned. A temptation is a device of Satan to entice you to sin.

Have you ever heard people who were going through a difficult time in their life say something like: "The Lord did this to me?" Or, "the Lord tempted me?" That simply isn't true, because the Lord is not capable of originating, instigating, or strategizing any kind of evil to tempt you in your life. The scripture above should make it very clear that God will never tempt any person with sin. All evil originates in the strategies of Satan. Sin never originates with God. All temptation comes from your enemy. He is the one who devises, the one who strategizes, and the one who plots against you to cause you to sin. Satan will challenge every positive claim that you make in your life. So, if you claim to be strong, Satan will see to it that you will be tempted to doubt it!

Just prior to Jesus entering into public ministry, He was tempted by Satan. In Matthew 4:1–11, you can follow the sequence of events that surrounded Jesus in His hour of temptation. The important point, however, is that this time of temptation has its strategic origin in the destructive mind of Satan. God was not tempting Jesus to break His fast, jump from the temple roof, or bow down and worship Satan. Moreover, Jesus, when tempted, used resources available to each one of us to resist temptation. As the Son of God, He could have played divine power, but instead chose to use the weapon we would use in future times. That weapon is none other than the "Sword of the Spirit," (Ephesians 6:17, NIV), or the spoken word of God. It did not fail Him, and it will not fail you.

A Temptation Can Also Be A Test

Although temptation does not come from God, sometimes He will allow temptation and use it as a test to prove us.

When Jodi was a teenager, she had just gotten her license and asked if she could drive a couple of friends to a school event. It was raining out, and she was a new driver. So Sheila and I were concerned. However, we gave her permission to go for it. Sure enough, she got in an accident that night. Thankfully, everyone involved was okay, but it turned into a valuable lesson for her. As her parents, we knew the danger, but we also knew that she wasn't going to be a teenager forever. She had to start doing things on her own. It's the same way with God. He may be involved in the process, but He allows us to take the wheel. First, He grants permission for you to be tried. Just like we gave permission to Jodi, you will not be tried or tested, as a child of God, without God permitting it to be done. God will observe you during the process of your testing so that He can prove you. God takes a temptation, and in His eyes, sees it as a test to prove what you can handle—what you are capable of. During God's observation, He is able to determine your potential and your personal ability. He then knows that when He pushes the "start" button on you and your purpose, you are not going to blow up on Him. You see: God wants to use you without losing you.

I have never created hardship for my daughter, Jodi. However, there have been times when I chose to not shield her from it. In those times, I observe her closely and am right there "coaching" her all the way. My goal is to see her matured by the hardship. I definitely do not want her to be overwhelmed or damaged. I want to see her made stronger by what she faces and conquers. In a similar way, God is not the creator of the hardships that we face. Sometimes, however, He will choose not to shield us from it and allow the temptation to also serve as a test, providing us with the opportunity to prove our potential.

God Needs To Verify That You Are "User-Friendly"

Do you remember the burning bush? In the book of Exodus, Moses looked into a burning bush that was ablaze with fire but not being consumed! God was using that bush. Do you know what condition that bush was in when God was through using it? It wasn't burnt up or consumed. It wasn't destroyed. When God was through using it, it returned right back to perfect health.

That's what God wants to do with you and I. He doesn't want to use you at the risk of losing you. He wants to use you without destroying you. He wants to know that when He uses you, you will be able to take it, and He wants to know that you can endure the heat of the situation.

Some people are zealous for God to use them. They dream of doing something significant in their lifetime. However, all they experience are problems. They blame their lack of success on the problems that they face. If they could realize that those problems are their opportunity to prove themselves, they would rejoice when facing them. Just like the book of James encourages us to do, "Consider it pure joy, my brothers, whenever you face trials of many kinds, because you know that the testing of your faith develops perseverance. Perseverance must finish its work so that you may be mature and complete, not lacking anything," (James 1:2–4, NIV).

James is saying that something positive is happening to us during our time of testing. Just as a product is never used until it is tested and proven, a person is never used until they are tested and proven. So, in the tests that you go through, your capabilities and your potential will be proven. What you can handle and what kind of positions you are suited for in life, these will all be proven in various tests along the way. In the following chapters, I am going to share with you nine major tests. These nine are the most common kinds of tests that will be encountered in the life of a Christ-follower. I've faced each and every one of them and still do repeatedly. I've faced some more than others. Some took more effort to pass. Some took longer for me to get through. I hope you can take the information and tools in this book and use them to help you to pass the tests of life and prove your personal God-given, exceptional potential!

P.S. Use the Think-it-Out section in each chapter to reflect on your own or with a small group. The Live-it-Out section is similar in that you can work through it as an individual or with a group study.

1
The Test of Small Things

THIS TEST COMES TO PROVE OUR POTENTIAL FOR GREATER OPPORTUNITIES.

The Question: Can You Handle More?

···

> *Whoever can be trusted with very little can also*
> *be trusted with much, and whoever is dishonest*
> *with very little will also be dishonest with much.*

Luke 16:10, NIV

Whether it's making the team, earning a diploma, getting your degree, receiving a promotion, building a business, growing a team, there are always smaller choices along the way that play a part in seeing God's plan come to fruition in our lives. There's actually a very famous story in the Bible that helps us to understand this test, and it comes from the backfields of Judea.

In this story, an unknown boy watches over his father's sheep day by day. As the days go by, the boy spends his time in the field practicing using his sling and playing music on his harp. Over time, he learns how to protect his father's sheep and kills not just a bear but also a lion with his slinging skills. Here's the thing: there were no cameras or crowds, but God was watching. One day, this unknown kid is given the task of delivering food to his older brothers on the battlefield, and in a matter of days, he goes from being an unknown shepherd boy to a giant-slaying national hero. The very same things that he practiced on the Judean hills while watching those sheep are the things that cleared a path for him to have an audience with the king.

It's the little things that make such a big difference. Because David got so good with sling throwing and kept his faith in the God he had heard about through the stories of people, he confidently took out Goliath when the opportunity finally came. Then, after hours of playing the harp on that same hillside, David had enough skills that the king sought him out to play for him. Being faithful with the little things over and over again opened new doors of opportunity for the young David. He wasn't perfect, but he eventually became the king that the prophet Samuel had prophesied him to become when he was that unknown boy in the fields with the sheep.

Jesus knew a thing or two about being faithful with the little things, and He taught about it more than once during His ministry. He could teach about it with so much conviction because He too had passed the test of small things time and again—even when it came to performing His first miracle. It wasn't a big crusade. Thousands didn't get saved with the revelation of His divinity. No one was healed. Instead, the first miracle recorded in Jesus' ministry was turning water into wine at the end of a wedding celebration when most of the guests probably wouldn't remember it even happened.

It was a small problem. But Jesus' mother asked Him to solve it, and it became an opportunity that set the course for thousands more miracles to take place during His time on earth.

A Problem, Whether Small Or Great,
Is Still An Opportunity

The year was 1986. At the age of 26, I had come to the Northwest to build a great church. As I eagerly accepted the opportunity to pastor my first church, I came face to face with Goliath-sized problems within the existing entity.

- An existing mortgage payment that was $4,000 dollars more than the church's total monthly income.
- A mountain of debt on accounts payable that had collectors calling and coming to our office demanding payment.
- A remaining congregation of less than 100 adults that had watched their congregation be separated by strife and decline drastically when their previous pastor resigned.
- A final splitting of the church when I became the pastor. (It's not a great morale boost when 20 percent walk out as you walk in!)

My wife, Sheila, was convinced that I was not thinking clearly. Why would I want her and our four-year-old daughter to leave our home, friends, and family to move to a little apartment with no furniture? From our home in St. Louis, there was no place we could go in the continental United States and be further away. When she asked me for an explanation, I had to be honest with her. And, my dad, who was also my pastor, deserved the same from me.

I could only say to them that I felt strongly that God was asking me to give myself completely to the cause of leading that church into growth and prosperity. There were other people who could, but I was young and unencumbered by other responsibilities at the point of the decision. I felt that God was reasoning with me by saying, "See what you can do with this opportunity." I realize this is not what most people say about the call of God, but that was my experience. For me, it was a matter of choice. What would I do with the opportunity was the real question I faced as we moved 2500 miles across the country.

Fast forward to August 1991. Every goal I had set out to accomplish when I began pastoring had now been accomplished:

· Our original debt of 11.2 million dollars was cut to less than half.

· We were doing much more than making a mortgage payment: We were supporting a staff with 30+ ministries operating in our church.

· Our church was multiplied ten times what it was when we came.

Anyone, who has known a degree of success, knows that success will create problems. Success, in fact, is not a destination but a journey. For those of us in ministry, growth creates the problem of needing more space. Space is necessary, not only to accommodate the ministry, but to continue growing the ministry. At that point in the

We cannot get to **where we want to go tomorrow** if we are always trying to bypass our today.

early '90s, we faced the problem of limited office space, classroom space, nursery space, and auditorium space. To solve the space problem, we had to face the lack of finances problem. How could we generate the necessary finances to solve the space problem? Anytime you are growing in family, business, or finances, you will continually encounter new problems. The bigger problems you solve, the bigger success you will enjoy.

Then fast forward five months to January 1992. We began to challenge the space problem by receiving our first building fund offering. The next few months were filled with blueprints, engineers, and planning meetings. As we faced our need to build, we had decided to look at a five-year plan to accommodate projected growth. While I was preparing to move into a building program, little did I know that God was preparing to offer me another opportunity of a lifetime.

Nearly a year later in December of 1992, the opportunity had presented itself. We could bypass the five year or more building project and move our ministry to the biggest wooden dome in North America just eight miles away from our current campus. The spacious, state-of-the-art 80,000 square feet People's Church had invited me to bring our congregation to their facility and merge our two churches together. The situation was incredibly familiar to our 1986 opportunity, only of much larger proportions:

- An existing Chapter 11 bankruptcy.
- A long list of accounts payable and unhappy creditors.

- A church congregation weakened and damaged by internal strife and financial struggles.
- A mortgage holder threatening to exercise his options at the end of the Chapter 11 reorganization period.
- The blending of two different congregations who had very different mindsets.
- The decision of what to do with the duplicate staff members.
- The replacement of the existing mortgage and placement with a new lender.
- Of course, somehow, balance the budget.

Here's the thing. It was a great opportunity to become the largest merger between two churches up until then, but it came with a price: a lot of hard work. The opportunity was so daunting that we could have easily missed it by shrinking back or thinking small, but there is a quote from journalist Ann Landers that fits what we were facing perfectly, "Opportunities are usually disguised as hard work, so most people don't recognize them." And, in the book of Ephesians it encourages us to, "Be very careful, then, how you live . . . making the most of every opportunity," (Ephesians 5:16, NIV). It was our opportunity to take, and we took it without looking back.

When we do our best with what God puts in front of us—big or small, hard or easy— we can be sure that we will be given more. This test asks you, "Can you handle more?" by allowing you to take responsibility for the things that

It's what we do with what we **have** that proves our potential to handle more.

are in your care right now, today. When we miss that truth and forget to take care of what is in our hand currently, we cannot get to the next level. We cannot get to where we want to go tomorrow if we are always trying to bypass our today.

Experience Required

In the corporate world, most companies prefer to promote within the organization by listing job opportunities on bulletin boards, in company papers, or making the opportunity available internally first. Alongside these opportunities, they will list the minimum qualifications, and the higher you go in an organization, the more experience is required with experience oftentimes valued above knowledge. For example, you can only learn so much about flying an airplane from a book or classroom. The real test of a pilot is their ability to fly the airplane. In fact, the Federal Aviation Administration, which issues pilots' licenses, requires a student pilot to log a minimum of 1500 flying[1] hours before being able to receive their license.

God's kingdom operates in a similar way with God observing us in real life situations. Many people sit in the seat every Sunday and read the Bible as a textbook. God's system for promotion, however, requires the student to log some experience in the application of what they learn in the manual, not just treat it like a task list. It's what we do with what we have that proves our potential to handle more. In the book of Matthew, it says, "You have been faithful with a few things; I will put you in charge of many things," (Matthew 25:23, NIV). When we are a good student pilot, we qualify to be a co-pilot, and only when we have done well as a co-pilot, are we a candidate to fly solo. This is a kingdom system of promotion.

I'm convinced that the passing of the previous tests in our ministry had positioned me as a candidate for a greater challenge. I knew again that God was saying, "Here's an opportunity. Are you interested?" I'm certain that God would not love me any less if I would have said that I would rather not face those challenges. I'm also certain that I was created for a specific kind of assignment and this new opportunity was tailor-made. Mordecai told his niece, Esther:

> *. . . who knows whether you have come to the kingdom for such a time as this?*

Esther 4:14, ESV

What if every time we faced a challenge, we said to ourselves, *"you were made for this!"* God made me to match the mission. It's true! God made you to match your mission. And God made you to match your mission. We are capable of doing all that God asks us to do. We don't have to do it, but if we choose to, He will empower us to succeed. On January 31, 1993, we had our first service as Covenant Celebration Church. A new church, birthed by merging two congregations, with a vision to take a new territory for the Kingdom of God. Our theme for our first year was

"Whatever It Takes." Every member of those two churches had to face challenges together if we were going to succeed:

- People showed patience with each other, in many cases preferring one another over themselves.
- People gave sacrificially of their finances to our Debt Destruction fund.
- People resisted the predictions of those prophesying our failure.
- One congregation welcomed another to "their house."
- The other congregation came with their families to a whole new environment: one Sunday in one building, the next Sunday in a different one.

By the end of the first year:

- The Chapter 11 was removed.
- The mortgage was placed with a new lender.
- The budget was balanced or as balanced as can be expected for a church who moves by faith.
- The congregations appeared to have always been together.
- The morale and confidence was high and the people were healthy.

We were promoted! The test was passed, not only by myself, but by the staff, leaders and the entire congregation. We were at a new level.

What Are You Doing With
What You Have?
. . . .

When I am considering giving a person an important responsibility in our ministry, I always want to look at how they are handling the responsibilities they already have. Red flags go up if I see:

- A low energy level in approaching their current responsibilities.
- The tendency to be late repeatedly, signaling that their schedule is out of control.
- Missing deadlines consistently.
- Their children not getting enough attention at home (this can be observed in the children's behavior usually).
- Unkempt yard, house, or automobile.
- Sloppy appearance or poor hygiene.

Many people see no connection between the kinds of things I'm referencing and how they would handle a more prestigious or public opportunity. My experience has been that the way a person handles their own personal responsibilities is an accurate indication of how they will handle ministry responsibilities. One indication to determine whether you are ready for increase, is how well you handle what you have. Some people will read this and quickly respond with, "I'm not doing too bad. I'm doing as well as most people do with what they have."

But here's the key: *most people* perform mediocre with the opportunities they have in life. What most people do creates the standard we call average. A lot of "average" people are offended by the reference to them as being average. However, few decide to actually be above average.

Another common mistake is for a person to conclude that they don't have what it takes to be above average, failing to realize that it's not what we have that is most important, but it's what we do with what we have. For example, most people assume that they must be born with a high IQ to excel in life. The truth, however, is that a high IQ can be a liability if it's not balanced by other thinking skills. Some of the most intelligent people in the world work for people of lesser IQ's. People of great intelligence are often kept average by poor attitudes, small thinking, or "paralysis of analysis" (when someone thinks so much that they don't make any decisions. They are stuck). So, being above average in the way you handle life's opportunities has very little to do with having a high IQ. In fact, brain power itself is included when we say that it's not what you have that's most important, but what you do with what you have.

Can I Handle Increase?

Accurate self-analysis is an important skill to increase in our lives. The people who make the most of life's opportunities are always looking for ways to improve themselves.

It's not what we have **that is most important,** but it's what we do with what we have.

These people know it's the little things that most people think don't make any difference that actually move them beyond mediocrity. Mediocre people even object to and protest when others (usually an employer or teacher) have the nerve to say that something minor in their mind (being on time, personal appearance, a positive attitude, good family life) has anything to do with them being a responsible person, employee, etc. They defend themselves by saying things like, "I get my job done."

This attitude is very common in people who don't realize that some effort, in the areas they consider irrelevant, will actually lift them from being a "C" class person to an "A" class person in their career or ministry. That "A" level is where God finds those who are ready for greater opportunity and can handle increase. If the person is at a "C" level with their current responsibilities, they would be overwhelmed and drop to an "F" status if given more responsibility. God does not want anyone to fail. He provides opportunities within our limitations, and ultimately, we decide if we can handle increase (not Him).

I can almost hear a defensive person saying, "God doesn't have a class rating. We're all an 'A' class to God." Of course, we are when it comes to His love for us. The topic we're discussing is the reward system God has for people. The Bible is clear: salvation is a free gift. God's love is unconditional. However, our works are rewarded both now and in eternity based on what we do with what we have. People who deny this are generally naïve or unproductive and are protecting their lack of productivity. These

The people who make the most of life's opportunities **are always looking for ways** to improve themselves.

people want a world system of equality that keeps all men and women at the same level of increase. Their system denies our God-given potential for ingenuity, creativity, and productivity. In that atmosphere, humanity's dominion mandate is harnessed and stifled. Human dignity and morale is destroyed when people have no system of reward for their labors.

Jesus Himself told several parables about slothful, unproductive servants. At one point in such a parable, the master ordered that the unproductive servant who had little, would lose what he had and that it would be given to a productive servant who already had much (Matthew 25:14–30). God's system of reward is not based on whether someone is a good person at heart. Neither is God's system of increase based on His love for humanity. Rather, both are based on what we do with what we have. This is the ultimate basis on which increase comes to our lives.

Tips To Help You Pass The Test Of Small Things

. . . .

1 **See your problems as opportunities.**
Ask yourself, "What's the solution?" Determine what you can do to solve the problem. Roll up your sleeves and do it. Don't avoid it. It's your opportunity in work clothes.

2 Treat small opportunities as if they were your doorway to greater ones.

Don't despise the responsibilities you have but be as diligent as you would if the whole world were watching, because God is watching and will promote you when you are proven.

3 Show motivation in the small things of your everyday life.

Honest self-analysis should point out areas where you can make a positive difference in yourself as well as your responsibilities. Dig into those areas without procrastination. Abraham Lincoln wrote in a letter, "I will study and prepare myself so when the opportunity comes I will be ready."[2] So, prepare yourself, and your day will come.

4 Make no excuses.

"Excuse-itis" is the disease of non-achievers. People who make excuses never excel with what they have. Give yourself no excuses for doing less than your best with your responsibilities.

Case Study: ABRAM (aka Abraham)

Let's do a case study of Abraham from the Bible. (Remember, he was called Abram first. Then his name changed to Abraham.) The questions below are based on Abraham's increase and are intended to help you assess your own readiness for increase.

Abram had become very wealthy in livestock and in silver and gold . . . But the land could not support them while they stayed together, for their possessions were so great that they were not able to stay together. And quarreling arose between Abram's herdsmen and the herdsmen of Lot.

Genesis 13:2, 6-7, NIV

- Increase means added responsibility: can I handle it?
- Increase can cause strife and tension between people: How well do I deal with it?

For example, when you rent a house, you call the landlord. When you own your own house, you are the landlord. When your ministry or business grows, you need more employees to answer the growing number of calls and needs. You may find tension in the changes necessary for staff to best accommodate the increase, because people are generally territorial in nature.

So, Abram said to Lot, 'Let's not have any quarreling between you and me, or between your herdsmen and mine, for we are brothers. Is not the whole land before you? Let's part company. If you go to the left, I'll go to the right; if you go to the right, I'll go to the left.'

Genesis 13:8-9, NIV

· Do I facilitate increase in my life?
· When increase comes, someone must find solutions to the problems that increase causes. Do I know the next needed step to accommodate the increase?

Increase will decrease unless we make room for it. Can you facilitate it or are you frustrated by it? If you are energized by it, you are a candidate for increase. You will find a way, like Abraham, to handle and facilitate the next level in your life, business, or ministry.

> *The Lord said to Abram after Lot had parted from him, 'Lift up your eyes from where you are and look north and south, east and west. All the land that you see I will give to you and your offspring forever. Go, walk through the length and breadth of the land, for I am giving it to you.'*

Genesis 13:14-15, 17, NIV

· Before you will have increase, you have to "see" it by imagining it. Ask yourself: "Do I see things that are not yet in existence, or can I only see what is a reality today?"
· Are you willing to dream of bigger, better things while not despising the smallness of what you have now? Some people can't do this without feeling discouragement with where they are today.

Notice Abraham had just been trying to accommodate his current increase, and God was inviting Him to get vision for future increase. Some would have resisted God's encouragement to "lift up your eyes . . . walk around in it and imagine increase coming," (Genesis 13:14, ESV). Some would not have been able to get a vision for increase. How about you? Can you "see" it?

If we want to pass the test of small things, first we need to recognize them and not overlook them. Each time we pass the test of small things, we experience increase. For instance, if you have been at the same company for a while and have done a good job at the tasks you were given, you have probably experienced promotion. Your job today is most likely a lot different than the job description you started with on your first day. It's because of a universal law God put into place at the creation of the world—sowing and reaping. If you sow commitment, perseverance, gratitude, and patience, you will get those things in return.

I'm here to tell you that God wants to see that the things He gives you to succeed, but He isn't going to give you too much too soon. Focus on the small things now and see what God will do through your life.

Think-it-Out

· · · · · · · · · · · · · ·

☐ What is a small thing in your life right now that you are going to take ownership of in this season?

....

☐ What is an example of a small thing that you accomplished in your life that opened doors to a bigger opportunity? (For example, doing a great job as a cashier at a coffee shop can open doors for shift manager and store manager.)

....

☐ Do you have a vision for increase? If yes, what inspired you to adopt that vision? If no, what steps could you take to "see" increase in your future?

....

☐ Is discipline something that comes naturally to you or do you have to fight for it? List some ways discipline can help you to pass this test.

....

....

....

....

Live-it-Out

. . . .

☐ How are you preparing yourself for your next opportunity? (For example, commit to one new habit each month and list out the habits you plan to acquire).

....

☐ Decide what the next step looks like to expand beyond your comfort zone and set a goal date to accomplish it.

....

☐ Memorize Luke 16:10 as a reminder when you're in the middle of the Test of Small Things.

Whoever can be trusted with very little can also be trusted with much, and whoever is dishonest with very little will also be dishonest with much.

Luke 16:10

2
The Motivation Test

THIS TEST COMES UPON A PERSON, WHO IS DOING THE RIGHT THING, TO PROVE WHY THEY ARE DOING WHAT THEY ARE DOING.

The Question: Are You Doing The
Right Thing For The Right Reason?
. . . .

He gave strict orders not to let anyone know about
this, and told them to give her something to eat.

Mark 5:43, NIV

Throughout His ministry, Jesus healed many people. A lot of them—most of them—couldn't give Him anything in return. He healed them simply to make them whole. Their healing was more about them and less about Him. In fact, several times when He performed a miracle He asked that the witnesses didn't tell anyone. More than fame or glory, Jesus kept His eye on the final prize of redeeming humanity on the cross and through His resurrection. He didn't allow temporary motivations to distract Him with the available and more immediate accolades along the way.

In the same passage of Mark 5 from the opening of this chapter, Jesus heals a woman in a crowded street and simply tells her to go in peace. Yet, when He raised a dead girl back to life, He gave strict orders for the family and witnesses not to tell anyone. It was His way of keeping the main thing, the main thing, and moving His ministry forward.

Motivation Is A Matter Of The Heart

Lasting motivation comes from the heart. People can be temporarily motivated by other people and things around them. Permanent, enduring motivation, however, can only come from within. The Bible tells us that the status of our heart will determine the outcomes of our lives. That is why in Proverbs, it says, "Above all else, guard your heart, for everything you do flows from it," (Proverbs 4:23, NIV).

Everything flows from it. In other words, it's the place from which our behavior and lifestyle are motivated. The source of our words and actions is our heart. The Bible pinpoints two ways that the content of our heart is revealed: the words we speak, and the way we spend our money.

First, when we are not on guard, the nature of our words will reveal the content of our heart. Jesus calls out the religious group of the day in Matthew, "You brood of vipers, how can you who are evil say anything good? For out of the overflow of the heart the mouth speaks," (Matthew 12:34, BSB).

Seeing the content of your heart can help you determine what is motivating you to do what you do. Many people today speak out of hurt that has not been healed. That hurt from a past relationship or bad experience is a motivating force in their life. By hearing them talk, you get an indication of why they don't trust others. Their motivation is unhealthy and will unfortunately hinder positive relationships in their future. These words, or slips of the tongue, reveal the critic in a person, the fantasies someone may have, the anger that is stored up on the inside, and the hurt left unresolved.

These are an indication of why people do what they do. Our words and actions will overflow out of what is going on in our hearts.

Secondly, the other way our heart is revealed according to the Bible by the way we spend our money. I haven't spent any money on mountain climbing equipment, parachuting, motorcycle riding, or snow skiing. While I have friends and family who invest their money in all of these, I wouldn't buy a parachute at 90 percent off the sale price, because I don't have any desire to jump out of an airplane. I have, on the other hand, invested in some golf clubs and hunting gear and travel gear. What motivates me to reach in my wallet may be different than what motivates you. However, something motivates all of us. Jesus said it like this, "For where your treasure is, there your heart will be also," (Matthew 6:21, NIV).

When it comes to the way we spend our money, the most powerful motivation comes from within. To know the motivations of a person's heart, simply look at where their "treasures" are going. People's treasures and their hearts are most likely in the same place.

There are other indicators of motivation, but one thing is sure—motivation is a matter of the heart. Because we are only able to see each other outwardly, it's easy to pass wrong judgment on other people. God, on the other hand, sees the heart: "...The Lord does not look at the things man looks at. Man looks at the outward appearance, but the Lord looks at the heart," (1 Samuel 16:7, NIV).

The Testing Of Your Motives

The thing I'd like you to know is that your motives will be tested on a regular basis. You will repeatedly have opportunities to stop and quit on something you're supposed to continue doing. If you want to go to the next level, don't give up. Remember, testing precedes promotion! The way to pass the Motivation Test is to keep doing what you're doing when you have no other reason to do it except that it's the right thing to do and you're supposed to keep doing it.

There have been countless times in my own life where I felt like there was no good reason to continue to pastor the church I pastor. On a few occasions, I was asked if I would consider pastoring a different church. What's interesting is that these kind of opportunities seem to come at times when I felt discouraged about pastoring in the Northwest. We are in one of the most unchurched regions. I'm not from here, and sometimes I have felt like a round peg in a square hole. The opportunities or thoughts about leaving seemed to be strongest when I felt no reason for staying. I've learned that the timing of these opportunities to leave are not a coincidence. That, at least in my case, the opportunity to leave was much more appealing when I felt less reason to stay. I would find myself thinking to myself, *People don't appreciate me . . . People in the Northwest are not ready*

to sacrifice and build the church God put in my heart . . . Our
church is stuck . . . I've done all I can do . . . I need a fresh place
and space where people will appreciate us, give, be committed,
and be excited to invite people to church.

In those seasons, when I felt like I had no good reason to stay is when I always ended up asking myself if any of the things I felt were the reason I was there in the first place. Was I there to be appreciated? Was I there because people wanted me there? Am I in the Northwest because it would be an easy place to build a church? Did God call me to our city because there were Christians waiting for a pastor they could celebrate? Is that why I was there?

This is an example of what it looks like when you go through a Motivation Test. In the time of testing, every beneficial reason for doing what you do will seem to be gone. Whether it's staying in your marriage, at the job God has you in, at the church you are meant to be in, or continuing to give, lead your small group, be faithful to what you've been ask to do. In everything that you have started and are meant to continue, there will be times when the motivation for doing what you do will come, so you can prove again that you do what you do when it's more convenient and tempting to quit. Now, the beauty in this is that every time you pass this test, the blessings, the joy, the appreciation of people, the respect of others, the fruit of your labors goes to another level! Without fail, when you see people who are experiencing longevity mixed with rewards and incredible blessings in life, they are people who have in the times of testing proved to do the right thing for the right reason

We're Not Stuck With Wrong Motives

Don't stop doing a right thing if wrong motives become evident. We're not stuck with wrong motives. One of the most common errors people make is to think that they are stuck with whatever is in their heart. When a person feels victimized by wrong motives, they will say, "I can't help it. That's just me. It will never change." I have good news for you. With God's help, you can change the content of your heart! God's promise in scripture is that when we turn to him, He will give us a new heart (Ezekiel 36:26). I've seen God do that for people, but it doesn't mean we don't have anything to do with the process and that God does it to us. It means that God does a work through us. He gives us the desire for a new life and gives us the ability to remove what we want to get rid of and replace it with what we desire to have in our heart.

For most people, the garage in their house is the place where stuff piles up: old stuff, stuff we don't know what to do with, stuff we're not even sure how we got. We all know that, if we just let it happen, we can accumulate all kinds of unwanted junk in the garage. Think of your heart as a garage. You may have some stuff you are emotionally attached to, but it's junk. You would be better off without it. There's old stuff from previous generations. They dumped it on you, and you continue to let it happen. There's stuff that so-called friends left you holding for them. You feel obligated to hold on to it. It's not your stuff, but they are your friends. So now you've accumulated some more extra baggage inside of you. The good news is that no matter what's been dumped into your heart, God wants to not only clear out the bad but also replace it with something so much better!

Approach your heart with a sense of ownership and responsibility. Ask God to help you renew your mind and heart of wrong motives and replace them with right ones. There's a right reason for doing every right thing we do. With God's help, we can consistently recognize and replace wrong motives with right ones. Don't stop doing a good thing if your reason for doing it is wrong. Rather, change your reason for doing it. You're not stuck with wrong motives.

Pay Attention To Those Things You Want to Have In Your Heart

The eyes and the ears are windows into the heart. What I mean by that is where you continually focus your attention on will enter your heart. But there's hope. As the content of your heart changes, your motives will change. We've already talked about the Proverb that tells us to guard our hearts, but there are a couple of verses before it that set it up perfectly, "My son, pay attention to what I say; turn your ear to my words. Do not let them out of your sight, keep them within your heart; for they are life to those who find them and health to one's whole body," (Proverbs 4:20–22).

All of us have suffered an injustice from another

person. When the incident occurs, we may find ourselves lying awake at night imagining how we will get revenge. Our mind races to rehearse the painful circumstance, nurse it, curse it, over and over again, and imagining the bad guy getting what they deserve.

At this stage, our attention is on the injustice, and so our motivation is to get even. Hopefully, our attention doesn't stay there. Hopefully, we intentionally shake it off and not dwell on it. As we move our attention to other things, our motivation to even the score will change.

After enough time passes, with little or no attention on the injustice, we may experience other motivations as we reflect back on the incident. Now we may be motivated to forgive them or have compassion on them, rather than being motivated to strangle them. How did this change? The motivation changed when we changed the focus of our attention from getting revenge to getting over it. We can choose what takes up residence in our heart by choosing where we focus our attention.

My Harvest Is In My Heart

In Washington State, we are proud of our apples. We have the world's best apples (to fully believe that, it helps to be from Washington). Imagine a farmer who has an apple orchard and is disappointed in the quality of the apples. They are infected, ugly, and no good. So what does he do? Would he say, "The barn is the problem. I need to paint the barn red, so I can grow healthy apples?" Or, would he say, "It's the pickup truck I'm driving. If I get a new model, I'll grow better apples?"

You and I both know the farmer would not react to a bad harvest of apples by painting the barn or buying a new truck. Yet, that's how a lot of people respond to the bad harvest of their lives. They place responsibility and blame for their problems on everything except the tree that produced the fruit! They blame other people, they blame the government, they go get a new wife or move to a different church. When a person doesn't deal with the unhealthy tree, the harvest won't change regardless of how many other changes they make. The harvest is not a product of any of those things, the harvest is a result of the heart!

The single most important element in the harvest of a person's future is the content of their heart. Think about it like this, Jesus compared a tree and its fruit with mankind and their actions in Matthew 12, "Make a tree good and its fruit will be good, or make a tree bad and its fruit will be bad, for a tree is recognized by its fruit . . . The good man brings good things out of the good stored up in him, and the evil man brings evil things out of the evil stored up in him," (Matthew 12:33,35, NIV). To understand this scripture, we must realize the meaning of the terms *fruit* and *tree*.

Fruit represents the ways of a person's life. It includes habits, behaviors, conversations, relationships, successes, or failures. While *Tree* represents the person's heart, it encompasses thoughts, attitudes, emotions, and wills. Jesus is teaching here that people are like trees, in that we produce on the outside based on what is on the inside. Just like healthy fruit is a sign of a healthy tree, likewise, good things in a person's life are a sign of good things in a person's heart.

Why Do You Do What You Do?

Motive defined is the compelling force or reason behind a person's actions. The following questions may appear simple on the surface. In reality, to assure complete accuracy, these questions must be answered in the face of adversity. At a time when every reason to continue is minimal or non-existent, we really discover our true motivation. Since you may not be in a time of testing right now, you should consider these questions as preparation for your eventual time of testing.

1 WHY DO WE GO TO CHURCH?

There are several benefits in belonging to the local church:

- A place to make friends with people who share our faith and values
- The opportunity to serve God and His people simultaneously

- The opportunity to partner in the cause of loving and building God's great church
- A place for our children to receive Christian education
- Fellowship, activities, and sports programs
- A support in times of personal crisis
- A place to have weddings, baby dedications, and funerals
- A place to learn Bible principles for life
- A place to be inspired and encouraged

All of these are legitimate personal benefits of belonging to a church. Sooner or later, however, every Christian will experience a season in their life when these benefits will feel insignificant or even be withdrawn temporarily. For example, a close church friend may move away. Things are not the same at church anymore. Besides that, some of the people you thought were friends have not been real friendly lately. You may find yourself not wanting to go to church. It's in that setting that our purpose in attending church must be recaptured.

God is hoping you will prove that your motivation is based on more than other people's actions. The right motivation for going to church is one of personal commitment and growth. In Hebrews, it says to "not giving up meeting together, as some are in the habit of doing, but let us encourage one another—and all the more as you see the Day approaching," (Hebrews 10:25, NIV). And, this verse in Psalm has always been a key verse for me when it comes to believing in and building the local church, ". . . planted in the house of the Lord, they will flourish in the courts of our God," (Psalm 92:13, NIV).

In church, as in any organization where humans are involved, there will always be human errors. As a pastor, I've regretted times when we've overlooked someone or taken a person for granted. One time, during a baby dedication weekend, our team left one family off of the list that I used to call the parents forward to dedicate their babies. Fortunately, this couple knew me well enough to know that it was nothing other than human error. Without anyone really noticing, they came forward with everyone else, and we dedicated their baby that day. I could not help but be thankful it had happened to a stable, secure couple. There are people who would have been offended by our mistake. In fact, people leave churches over things like that all the time. When they do so, they miss out on one of God's intentions for putting us together in the first place. God knew we would have personality differences, human errors, disagreements, and conflicts.

A major element of our personal development is accomplished by learning how to work through differences, while maintaining a spirit of unity. Our character is strengthened when we get past our fragile feelings, drop our guard and "lock into" the church. This generation approaches church with a consumer mentality. Unfortunately, this keeps some people shopping for a better deal.

Although it's important to consider your needs

when looking for a home church, you must also realize that your relationship with the church is one of giving and receiving. There are seasons when you will be giving more than receiving. You will tend to underestimate the value of the church in your life during that time. But remember, every healthy relationship must have seasons of both giving and receiving.

If someone left our church today, I would still be preaching next weekend. They may not show up, but I'll still be doing what God has called me to do. You need to have that same kind of stick-to-it mentality in your church commitment, so your motivation can be proven. I am not a pastor so that I can get a pat on the back. I don't preach on the weekend to hear people say, "Pastor, that was a great message!" When no one compliments me, I don't think to myself, "I've had it with these people. I'm not going to preach again!" You have to be doing ministry for purposes greater than those trivial things. And, I hope you can get planted in a local church for purposes greater than just what is in it for you.

2 WHY DO WE PRAY IN PUBLIC?

Have you ever asked yourself this question? In more than 30 years of ministry, I have heard all kinds of questions about prayer. When to do it, how to do it, where to do it . . . honestly, it is less about the logistics and more about the why behind the what. People who pray or worship in public and fail to do so in private have reason to check their motives.

And when you pray, do not be like the hypocrites, for they love to pray standing in the synagogues and on the street corners to be seen by others. Truly I tell you, they have received their reward in full. But when you pray, go into your room, close the door, and pray to your Father, who is unseen. Then your Father, who sees what is done in secret, will reward you.

Matthew 6:5-6, NIV

A lot of people think that the above verse means that we shouldn't pray in public. However, Jesus is not against public prayer and worship. He is challenging the religious group called the Pharisees to stop public worship that is motivated only by a desire to impress others. His challenge is to persuade them to worship for the right reason.

Some people falsely judge expression-filled worship as being a show performed for people. Yet, the Bible teaches congregational praise and worship. The Bible calls us to expression-filled corporate worship. Take a look at this next verse and consider all the potential ways we are encouraged to worship:

Praise the Lord. Praise God in His sanctuary;
praise Him in His mighty heavens. Praise Him
for His acts of power; praise Him for His sur-
passing greatness. Praise Him with the sounding
of the trumpet, praise Him with the harp and
lyre, praise Him with tambourine and dancing,
praise Him with the strings and flute, praise
Him with the clash of cymbals, praise Him with
resounding cymbals. Let everything that has
breath praise the Lord. Praise the Lord.

Psalm 150:1-6, NIV

I believe that the next generation and the generation after that not only needs to see us worship, they need to hear us pray. Our churches should be filled with expressive songs that point people to worshipping Jesus. When Christ-followers come together to worship and pray, atmospheres are created where people can have personal encounters with the God we serve. The challenge of public prayer, worship and praise is to do it with the right motives.

3 WHY DO I GIVE?

In the Old Testament, the Israelites brought the best unspotted lamb they owned, only to watch it go up in smoke while burning at an altar. The next time you give, remember that God wants us to give our best regardless of

Are you doing the right thing **for the right reasons?**

whether He uses it like we want Him to use it or not. What would you do if next weekend your pastor said, "Bring your offering so we can burn it."? Most people would say, "No way! I want you to use my money wisely, or you won't get any tithe and offering from me."

Although I do agree that we should practice good stewardship with kingdom finances, the issue we're looking at is one of motivation. We can desire to see ministries be good money managers, but should never make our tithe and offering a conditional practice. You know, the "I'll give if you will do what I want you to do" attitude. I've had several opportunities to receive offerings with strings attached that I have not accepted. Generally, if the giver's motivation is right, they will release the control of the offering when they give the offering.

I realize that sometimes it's appropriate to designate offerings for a specific cause. There's nothing wrong with that, when offerings are being received for that purpose. However, some people don't give generously to advance God's kingdom, but rather exchange their tithe or offering for a specific thing they desire. In other words, they get something back in exchange for a donation. Tithing and general offerings should be given systematically for your church to use in alignment with the vision of the pastors and leaders. They become responsible before God for stewardship of the tithe and offerings. We receive our blessings, as givers, simply based on our giving.

The Reason I Do What I Do Will
Ultimately Determine What I Do

. . . .

Remember, the definition of motive is *the compelling force behind our actions.* In other words, the reason I do what I do will ultimately determine what I do.

For example, people who attend church for the wrong reasons eventually will no longer attend church. I've watched men come to church to make a girlfriend happy. Eventually, unless they find a right reason for attending, they stop coming. The motivation for attending church is tested when they get married or break off the relationship. He was attending church for her when it was required to be a candidate for marriage. Now that they aren't together anymore, the original motivation does not exist. So, the real reason for going will now determine what he will do. In this case, without a new reason for going, he is no longer motivated to attend.

Another example is people who get married for the wrong reasons must find a right reason for staying together if they expect it to last a lifetime. An unexpected pregnancy has caused many couples to feel as if they had to get married. Two wrongs don't make a right. Other individuals get married for fear they may not get another chance. Temporary reasons motivating these kinds of marriages today will not continue to motivate the marriage forever. Ultimately, if these people do not find a right basis for their marriage, they end up confessing to each other, counselors, and pastors why they married in the first place. If you listen to them, the amazing thing is that often the original reason they got married is now the reason for divorce! They say, "I only married because I was pregnant," or "I felt pressure to marry."

Passing the motivation test is important to get to the heart of the matter. Are you doing the right thing for the right reason? Because, the reason you do what you do will ultimately determine what you do.

Playing Games

Game playing is a favorite pastime in our society. It matches the wit, intelligence, courage, strength, and endurance of people. In fact, we like games so much we spend millions of dollars on stadiums, arenas, television airtime, skilled players, and athletes, so we can have games. We have game shows, games stores, even games based on games.

Game playing can be fun, challenging, and harmless when on a playing field or a game board. However, when the mentality of a game spills over into life, it can damage a family, career, reputation, health, and even a relationship with God. There are three reasons people drift into game playing on the field of life.

1 ˙ PEOPLE PLAY GAMES TO AVOID FACING REALITY.

People play emotional and mental games to avoid facing an unwanted reality. This game is most commonly called denial. The basic strategy is, "If I ignore the problem and pretend it doesn't exist, it will go away." Recently, someone mentioned to me that the tire on my car looked flat. Now, I could have pretended that it wasn't, but that wouldn't have changed anything. When I got up the next day, the tire would still be flat.

Don't consider the recognition of your flat tire as compounding the problem. You already have a problem and recognizing it is the first step toward a solution. In my situation, I was able to do some temporary fixing by putting air in the tire and delaying the actual repair. This is possible and sometimes appropriate with situations in life. In the meantime, I was looking at my calendar and planning the best time to get it fixed. I was delaying the confrontation, but not ignoring it. Make sure your delays are not a denial, because the tire will not get fixed on its own.

2 PEOPLE PLAY GAMES TO MAKE THEMSELVES APPEAR DIFFERENT THAN THEY ARE.

Someone once said, "A person is in danger of complete failure when it becomes more important to keep a secret than to solve a problem." For example, many men today find it difficult to receive counsel for their marriage. The male ego struggles with letting anyone know that he needs help. Unfortunately, many troubled relationships never improve because secret keeping is the primary motivation rather than problem solving. "Keeping up the image" has been the downfall of many businesses, churches and homes.

3 PEOPLE PLAY GAMES TO AVOID PARTICIPATION.

Many of the games people play are learned early in life. A ten-year-old child can't tell his parents, "Look, I don't want to go to school today. I'm tired, and I want the day off." So, since that won't get him anywhere, he must put on his "sick" face and "sick" voice and murmur, "I don't feel good today." If executed well, this kind of acting could get him out of going to school. In this same way, adults play games to avoid going to the in-laws' house, Junior's ball game, or another undesirable event. Oftentimes, just pretending you don't see someone can get you out of having to speak to them.

When a person's actions are motivated by these shallow, psychological games, life will be fragile, at best. Authenticity and a commitment to enduring principles are the highest level of motivation. These alone, guarantee real, genuine, Godly and lasting success.

Passing the test of motivation requires you to look inwardly to really assess why you do what you do, because if you're in it for the wrong reasons, God won't elevate you to where you're motivated to go.

Think-it-Out
. . . .

☐ Why do you go to church?

....

☐ Do you often expect an exchange when it comes to giving tithes and offering?

....

☐ If things don't go the way you planned, do you run away or stay the course?

....

☐ How does "the reason you do what you do will ultimately determine what you do" resonate with you?

....

☐ If God told you today that He wanted you to go in a completely different direction that takes you out of your comfort zone, would you? Why or why not?

....

☐ Write out why you do what you do. What's the reason behind your job, your relationships, your ministry, etc.

....

....

....

Live-it-Out
. . . .

☐ This week, make a commitment to be very intentional about what motivates you. Assess if you are healthy or unhealthy in this area and make necessary changes in perspective.

☐ Take time to do a heart check. What's flowing from your heart and does it align with scripture?

☐ Memorize Colossians 3:23 and think about how it applies to what motivates you.

Whatever you do, work at it with all your heart,
as working for the Lord, not for human masters.

Colossians 3:23

3
The Credibility Test

**THIS TEST PROVES
OUR RELIABILITY AND
TRUSTWORTHINESS.**

The Question: Can Others Count On You And Trust You With The Opportunities Given To You?

. . . .

And Jesus grew in wisdom and stature, and in favor with God and man.

Luke 2:52, NIV

A ll of us, at one point in our lives, have lost and gained credibility. Maybe you made a mistake that lost the trust of people around you, or perhaps you spent years in school to get a degree so that you could be reliable in a field. If so, then you know what it's like to lose credibility and you also know what it's like to gain credibility. There's a reason this test is so important—**your ability to gain and maintain credibility is what opens the door to your next opportunity.**

For example, if a person is interested in being hired for a specific career position, they must first establish credibility with the person who is doing the hiring. Passing the test will mean a promotion into the new career. When you stop and consider this, you can't help but realize that most, if not all, of life's promotions occur after you've passed some form of credibility test. **Credibility is a combination of what you do, who you are, and how others view you.**

Have you ever been in a public place and noticed

someone trying to get a good picture? I've seen people standing on chairs to get the best shot of their coffee. In the world of social media, perception can be far from reality, because we live in a time where people go to great lengths to create an image that people will like. But what happens when reality is different than your news feed? Either you lose credibility, or someone you follow loses credibility with you. When someone has a credibility problem, it may have more to do with perception than it does with facts.

Our desire for people to see us as credible is biblical. We see that even in Jesus' life and ministry He "... grew in wisdom and stature, and in favor with God and men," (Luke 2:52, NIV). In fact, this one verse is really all we know about a season of Jesus' life. From the time He was about 12-years-old and got "lost" in the temple, until we see Him back on the scene being baptized by His cousin, he was steadily building credibility in His everyday life. Part of growing and increasing in life is to grow and increase in favor with God and man. This doesn't happen overnight, but over a series of moments and decisions.

For example, a man claiming to be a tailor can go to tailor school, open a tailor shop, and hang a sign that identifies him as a tailor. The real proof that he is indeed a tailor, however, is when he has customers. In fact, without customers, eventually the sign will come down and the shop will close. There will be no tailor shop, and there will be no tailor. The hope for the wannabe tailor is to establish credibility, not only as a tailor but as an exceptional one. That credibility is essential in the proving of his potential.

Part of growing in life is to increase in **favor with God** and man.

No One Else Can Earn Your Credibility

To further the example of a tailor, let's imagine that the tailor shop is now established and the tailor has a great reputation. One evening, a stranger walks into the shop and asks if he could be allowed to do some tailoring of his own in the tailor's shop. "In fact," he says, "would it be possible for me to begin tomorrow morning?" All of the credibility earned by the tailor's shop is insufficient to make this newcomer a tailor. He will only be a tailor if others regard him as being one (including the owner of the shop). Credibility cannot just be transferred. It must be earned. The aspiring tailor may first only have to earn it with the owner, but eventually, his credibility will have to extend beyond that if he is going to have repeat customers. Even when we receive mentoring and learn from those who have gone before us, each of us will eventually pass or fail our own credibility test.

THERE ARE THREE FORMS OF CREDIBILITY THAT CONTRIBUTE TO THE PROVING OF YOUR PERSONAL POTENTIAL:

1 The Credibility of Competence
2 The Credibility of Personality
3 The Credibility of Character

Consider a musician to evaluate these three components. When it comes to competence, can she play the guitar? If so, how well? If we look at personality, is she enjoyable to work with? Does she have a God-like attitude? Lastly, her character should be put to question. Does she show up when she says she will? Can I count on her? Let's take a more in-depth look at all three.

Credibility Of Competence

Competence is about people knowing that you know what you're doing, which allows them to trust you in your work. This credibility is earned when you are proven to have:

- *The necessary skills for the role you are in.* Examples: communication, organization, technical skills, leadership, etc.
- *The necessary knowledge for the role you are in.* Examples: education, experience, or natural instincts.
- *The right kind of habits for the role you are in.* Examples: some people are required to stay in good physical condition and mental alertness to be competent for their job. Police officers, airline pilots, and air traffic controllers are required to maintain habits of discipline. A variance from this will endanger their credibility for competence.

One of the things God wants to know before He

places you in your calling is that you can do the job. God doesn't set us up for failure. We may set ourselves up to fail, but God will not give us more responsibility than we can handle. This is why we should not force doors open in our own lives, but rather work in God's timing. One of the Proverbs says, "In their hearts humans plan their course, but the Lord establishes their steps," (Proverbs 16:9, NIV). You may know where you are going in life, but if you attempt to go ahead of schedule, you will find yourself incompetent and suffering the loss of credibility.

The equipping of oneself, so that you remain competent, is an ongoing, never-ending task. What may have been considered fresh and cutting edge just five years ago, may now be outdated and inefficient. Methods and skills are constantly being improved in every area of life. Yesterday's success may be applauded, respected, or honored, but competence is credibility based on what you can do today. This credibility is earned by performance, not by respect, love, honesty, courage, or other important virtues.

Some people expect this kind of credibility to be automatically extended to them on the basis of friendship. They reason that friends who have hiring power should hire friends who are unemployed based on "friends help friends." This kind of reasoning overlooks the importance of competence as well as other kinds of credibility. Think about it this way: a father denying his ten-year-old son the opportunity to drive his car. It may appear to the child that, "if Dad really loved me, he would let me drive the car."

Competence is credibility

based on what you can do today.

Reality, however, is that dad can still love his son very much and judge him as being untrained, unskilled, or not ready, and presently incompetent to drive the car. It's the same today for you and I in the areas that we need to grow in. Whatever we strive for or attempt to achieve in life can only happen by earning the credibility of competence.

- Do you want to build houses?
- Do you want to do people's taxes?
- Do you want to be an educator?
- Do you want to be a church leader?
- Do you want to start and build a business?
- Do you want to plant a church?
- Do you want to practice law?
- Do you want to make food people will love to eat?
- Do you want to fly airplanes?
- Do you want to be a counselor?
- Do you want to lead a Bible study?

The question is what are you doing today to be able to do the things God has asked you to do? It may be time to invest in learning a new skill, asking questions, and learning from an expert in your field of choice. Or it may simply mean making the time to refine a skill.

Credibility Of Personality

. . . .

You've probably seen a movie with an actor or actress who really felt relatable to you. Maybe you watched them play a doctor or a crime solver. You may have had thoughts that they seem down-to-earth or that that they actually know what they are doing. What you're recognizing is their ability to use their personality to gain credibility with you. Your personality can make a permanent impression on all of us, either positive or negative. This credibility is not based on talent, skill, or character. It's established rather on a person's traits. Politicians win thousands, even millions, of votes based on their personality. This credibility is one that we may not want to give much regard to, especially by itself. However, a pleasing personality is a tremendous aid in establishing our credibility with other people. Those who pass it off as unimportant will limit their own potential in life. Those who consider it to be the only form of credibility that is important will eventually suffer the loss of life's gains. Here's how your personality can help with your credibility:

- *Having a positive effect on others when they are in our presence.* They feel our attitude, and it feels good.
- *Practicing common courtesy toward others.* A smile, good manners, genuine concern for them, hospitality, openness, etc. You start to build relationships with those around you.

Many people are hindered in life by an unpleasant personality. They may have a servant's heart and great intentions, but their personality is "*blah*." People are uncomfortable around them and may even avoid being with them. In ministry, I've seen individuals who didn't realize what happened when they joined a ministry team and soon became the only person on the team. Everyone else was repelled by this one individual's personality. If a person is blind to this, they go through life repelling people and never knowing why.

Negativity is the chief cause for a person with an unpleasant personality. A negative personality will bring heaviness to a light and enjoyable conversation. A negative personality sees only problems and not solutions. Since everyone has their own share of challenges, people consciously or subconsciously avoid exposure to additional negativity in their lives. So if you're looking at the people around you and you're realizing how negative they are, it's a sure sign that you may be negative too. Because positive people want to be around other positive people. The way we identify and avoid people who have negative personalities provides the basis for the loss of their personality credibility. Listed below are six questions to ask yourself to help you recognize negativity in your own life.

A Check-Up From The Neck Up

....

1 **What do I think about most?**
- Thoughts that trouble me or make me irritable?
- Thoughts that encourage me and make me feel confident?

2 **How do I respond to problems or difficulties?**
- Am I challenged or discouraged?
- Do I solve or do I compound problems?

3 **What do I do when I hear negative feedback?**
- A negative person quickly attaches negative feedback to their self-worth and becomes defensive.
- A positive person can separate the feedback from their self-worth, making them more objective and able to improve.

4 How comfortable am I with failure or defeat?

· Positive people have glitches, mistakes, or setbacks, but not failures or defeat.

· Negative people, on the other hand, expect failure, and they get it.

5 What kind of people do I get along well with?

· Anyone? What are they like (be honest)? Are they confident, encouraging, successful?

6 How do I respond to positive information?

· Do books, literature, and speeches tend to inspire and motivate me?

· Am I critical of people who have experienced success?

· Do I accept the value of faith and confidence for my life, or do I disregard it as shallow and unimportant?

Negative people always pride themselves on being more of a realist than the positive people around them. A negative person usually fails to recognize the difference between noticing the negative and being negative. A positive personality can see a headline in the news that says, "the economy is slumping" without having to elaborate on it or get depressed by it. A negative personality, however, will make it the headline of their day and offer no encouragement to those around them.

When the disease of negativity grows within a person, it's easy to deny reality. A negative personality is blind to life's blessings and God's promises. A negative personality has a different reality than a positive personality. Neither reality is more realistic than the other. They are both very real to the individual and to life. Life has pain, hardship, and problems. Life also has joy, pleasure, and blessings. To have a positive personality, one does not have to deny life's realities, but simply focus on the good. The Apostle Paul wrote in his letter to the church at Philippi, "Finally, brothers, whatever is true, whatever is noble, whatever is right, whatever is pure, whatever is lovely, whatever is admirable—if anything is excellent or praiseworthy—think about such things," (Philippians 4:8, NIV).

Some other tips for earning credibility:

· Manage your moods.
· Smile often with your face and your voice.

- Greet others without waiting to be greeted first.
- See the people around you as having high value.
- Speak fluently, words of blessing and inspiration to others.
- Practice motivational maintenance of your own life (get plenty of rest, exercise, and faith food).

Credibility Of Character

I was speaking in a Sunday morning service when I said, "If your employer is demanding that you do something that violates your conscience, go in tomorrow and quit your job." There was a man in the audience that day who believed that was a direct word for him, and he quit work on Monday. He then wrote a letter to me:

Dear Pastor,

Three Sundays ago, my wife and I visited Champions Centre for the very first time. After you had given your message, you spoke out a word, that if anyone was in a job in which it caused them to lie, they needed to quit immediately and specifically to go in and resign on Monday morning. Well, that word was for me! For the last six months, I have been struggling over the lying I was doing in order to sell advertising for my company. Primarily, I did not believe in the program at all. Being afraid to quit, with only 200 dollars in my account, a wife, and two kids to support, I went and quit my job on Monday. Immediately, I went to look for a new job. The first week, I applied for 14 jobs and had seven interviews. All I got was four hours of work in a warehouse with a temp job company. But that earned us enough money to keep going on for the next week.

Week two, I put in seven resumes, had three interviews, and worked one day in a sausage factory for another temp job company. That again earned us enough money to keep going on for the next week.

The following Wednesday, I landed a new job. Not any job, but one that was beyond what I could have hoped for. Instead of straight commission, I received a salary plus commission. I was offered medical benefits, retirement, and projected earnings of almost twice the amount I was previously earning. Plus, a nice trip to Florida for training!

I just wanted to let you know, because I thought God should get all the glory, for He is faithful to His Word.

There were two obvious tests in this experience. First, there was the authority test, and second, there was the credibility of character test. John made a decision to withdraw from the authority that was placing him in a position that compromised his character. In making this decision, John was passing the test and promotion was sure to follow. The promotion did not come immediately, but John maintained character in a difficult circumstance. This is where some people lose their reward by becoming impatient and breaking character.

Going back to my example of actors and actresses, there is nothing more challenging than a live stage performance. On television, you can cut, paste, edit, and shoot again until you get a scene perfect. But in live theater, the show must go on!

Actors can forget lines, come on stage at the wrong scene, or trip and fall down at exactly the wrong moment. Good actors, however, know one important response to the undesirable interruption: *stay in character!* It's the ability to stay on course and continue with the scene as if nothing happened. The predetermined character, being played by an actor, cannot be compromised regardless of what happens around him. The sign of a good actor is when they don't break character in difficult situations.

Likewise, our character ethics are never known until they are tested. We may have good intentions, but intentions are not the same as good character. Good character is the moral strength to maintain our pre-planned course of good intentions in the moment of opposition. At that

Good character is the moral strength to maintain our pre-planned course of good intentions in the moment of opposition.

specific moment, it is tempting to break character. The circumstances seem to justify it. The weak will break and compromise. Only the strong survive. The difference between maintaining stage character and moral character is that moral character is often challenged in private, while stage character is challenged in public. Perhaps the greatest opponent to moral and ethical character is the voice that whispers, "Nobody will ever know. What could it possibly hurt?" It's in that moment of potential compromise that we must be true to ourselves. When we are true to ourselves, we pass the greatest character test of all. It's only then when we are honest with ourselves that we are prepared to be honest with God and other people.

We see this in the story of David when a prophet named Nathan confronted him with his sin (2 Samuel 12). First, Nathan had to wake David up from an obvious state of denial. David, who was a man after God's own heart, had apparently justified his sin of adultery with Bathsheba in his own mind. It appears that he was moving on with his life as if nothing had happened. Here's the truth, denial blocks out the truth within us.

Someone who is in denial often does not realize it, and they genuinely fail to acknowledge an obvious reality. This person has a blind spot, which hinders their perspective. Nathan's approach to David was to tell him a parable about a rich man, who thought he had much, took the only small lamb that a poor man had. David, who was king, thought that Nathan was referring to a real incident within his kingdom and demanded to know who had done such a terrible thing. While David's mind was open to injustice, Nathan rifled back the answer, "David, you are the man!" Imagine how David felt at that instant. Like taking a powerful slap on the face, he is shocked by this confrontation. It was in this moment, when truth was unveiled, that David's future would be decided.

However, David was faced with the reality that all of us face: allowing our pride to be a "cover up" when our character is at stake. Those who choose to cover up, go back into denial. Fortunately, David did not choose to cover up his moral failure. He did not become defensive and guarded. He welcomed truth and allowed it to speak. He listened with his heart to the evidence that was presented to him that day. When his wrongs were revealed to him, David repented. This was a great day in the life of David. Rather than losing credibility, he gained it. His ability to be honest with himself was a sign of great character.

His blind spot was torn away, and David was seeing clearly again. It was then, in the midst of his own failure, that David did not make excuses. He did not blame others. He chose to be authentic and honest. This level of self-honesty enabled him to be honest with God. Psalm 51 records that prayer. Notice his understanding of his own need for inner truth:

Have mercy on me, O God, according to your unfailing love; according to your great compassion, blot out my transgressions.

*Surely you desire truth in the inner parts; you
teach me wisdom in the inmost place. Cleanse me
with hyssop, and I will be clean; wash me, and I
will be whiter than snow.*

*Create in me a pure heart, O God, and renew a
steadfast spirit within me. Do not cast me from
your presence or take your Holy Spirit from me.
Restore to me the joy of your salvation and grant
me a willing spirit, to sustain me."*

Psalm 51:1, 6-7, 10-12, NIV

Inside-Out Living

In the church world, there's a school of thought that
struggles with the idea of Christians wanting to succeed
in life. The common question that goes along with this
thought is, "What's the difference in the world's approach
to success and the message coming from the church?" But
what this question misses is the approach. The world approaches success from the outside-in, while God's approach
is from the inside-out. God Himself has given us formulas
for success: "Do not let this Book of the Law depart from
your mouth; meditate on it day and night, so that you may
be careful to do everything written in it. Then you will be
prosperous and successful," (Joshua 1:8, NIV).

This is shown in the example of the man who quit his

job so that his character was not compromised. He's a prime example of "inside-out" living. The worldly approach would have been to place higher value on keeping the job than on telling the truth. This inverted approach to success creates an environment for eventual failure. God's plan for success is to consistently draw our attention to our own character. By focusing on the ethics of our heart, we can be assured that good things will come out of our lives. As I mentioned in the motivation test, Jesus says this in Matthew 12:35, "The good man brings good things out of the good stored up in him . . ." This is inside-out living in a nutshell.

Credibility Leads To Influence

When a person passes the credibility test, they enlarge their sphere of influence. Your level of influence right now is dependent on the degree to which you have earned credibility with people. As Christ-followers, it's important that we increase our influence in society. The only way this will happen is if we actively increase our credibility as following after Christ's example. The world has seen the "dirty laundry" of Christian leaders and all of us have dealt with a loss of credibility. Society doesn't understand God's grace and gift of righteousness like we do. Society only understands credibility or lack thereof. God may never create perfect people, but He is going to encourage people to pass the credibility test and have growing influence on our world. We gain this credibility by:

- Becoming equipped with the thoughts
  and ways of God.
- Living with faith-filled minds, hearts, and faces.
- Showing integrity and ethics in our relationships.
- Modeling parenthood and training our children.
- By building strong marriages.
- Succeeding in our chosen careers and vocations.
- Helping people who are hurting and begin to
  heal our world.
- By prospering and managing our finances well.

These very real accomplishments in the lives of Christians will give credibility, and will also increase our influence on this earth. The valuable result is that we will honor and glorify our Father[3] in heaven. Let's pass this test!

Think-it-Out
. . . .

☐ If you could rate your credibility on a scale of 1–10, what score would you give it? Why?

....

☐ What are some steps you can take today to build your credibility?

....

☐ Where do you want to be in five years? What are you doing today to be able to do the things God has planned for you to do in your future?

....

☐ Write down which area needs the most improvement: competence, personality, or character. Why?

....

....

....

....

....

Live-it-Out
. . . .

☐ What steps can you take to improve your credibility when it comes to competence, personality, and character?

....

☐ Ask God to reveal to you the things that you are in denial about.

....

☐ Find someone you can trust and ask them for feedback about your character. Listen with an open mind, and take steps to improve.

....

☐ Read and memorize Proverbs 10:9 and consider if you walk securely in your own credibility.

Whoever walks in integrity walks securely, but whoever takes crooked paths will be found out.

Proverbs 10:9

4
The Wilderness
Test

THIS TEST COMES IN THE FORM OF A DROUGHT OR DRY SEASON AND WILL PROVE YOUR POTENTIAL TO MAKE THE CHANGES NECESSARY TO ENTER THE NEXT LEVEL OF PROSPERITY IN YOUR LIFE.

The Question: Are You Ready To Make The Change That Progress Requires Of You?

. . . .

Then Jesus was led by the Spirit into the wilderness to be tempted by the devil.

Matthew 4:1, NIV

There will be times when questions are many and answers are few, and times when God's "felt" presence seems so far away. You survive, but you don't thrive. The blessings of abundance are beyond this place. Your supply does not match your demand. Before Jesus officially began His ministry, He had His own wilderness experience. It was just after He was baptized by His cousin, John. He then entered the wilderness to fast for 40 days and 40 nights. Even Jesus was tempted to lose Himself in the wilderness. He felt distant to God and had to rely on His knowledge of God and His faith to pull Him through.

In one of the greatest stories of the Bible, the people we know as the children of Israel (or Israelites) got stuck and were unable to transition into a new and better place. They had become *sentimentally attached* to the life they had known. They would not let go of their lives in Egypt. To us, reading the story it seems ridiculous. A fresh, new life awaits them on the other side of the wilderness, but to them, surrendering Egypt was a big deal. Letting go of the old is a big deal to most people today.

It is estimated in the Great Exodus, that as many as five million Israelites left Egypt to go to the "Promised Land." While en route to possessing their promised land, the people had to pass through the wilderness. The wilderness was a necessary part of the journey. It was between them and their destination. In Deuteronomy, it summarizes their experience, "He led you through the vast and dreadful desert, that thirsty and waterless land with its venomous snakes and scorpions. He brought you water out of hard rock. He gave you manna to eat in the desert, something your ancestors had never known, to humble and to test you so that in the end, it might go well with you," (Deuteronomy 8:15–16, NIV).

An estimated 11-day journey ended up taking 40 years. I think God knew that generation who grew up in Egypt as slaves had left Egypt physically, but the mentality of Egypt and slavery was still inside them. It was a serious hindrance to the ongoing, generational work that God wanted to do. An entire generation died in the wilderness and never experienced the Promised Land. Let's not be like that generation—they didn't realize that testing precedes promotion—let's pass the Wilderness Test!

Similar to Jesus and the Israelites, our journey of progress will include some "dry" or wilderness-like places that is between the land of not enough and the land of more than enough. It's the place between dependence and independence. It's what we go through when we leave the place of bondage and move toward freedom. The wilderness is what you will travel through if you attempt to go from the place of poverty to the place of plenty.

It's easy to want to stay where you're at, to see your life with a lid that limits the possibility of progress in your future. The best news for you is to know that feeling is common to everyone who is attempting to move their life forward. There will always be resistance between where you are and where you are going. The resistance doesn't mean you have to settle there. You may be in a season of just getting by and feel destined to a lifetime of staying in the land of just enough. Perhaps, you're too afraid of the wilderness to even consider what's on the other side. You might be in the middle of this test, and you feel crippled to take another step even if it means finding a fresh opportunity and a better life beyond the difficult place you've been living in. The reality is we can't get to the new—the better—without going through the wilderness, and your ability to pass this test is determined by your dependence on God. He wants you to move forward. He wants you to overcome. Don't hold onto the past. Let it go and look into the future. Trust God to do new and better things in your future than in your past. God is not just a God of the past. He's the God of the future.

Your response to the wilderness will **determine how long** you stay in the wilderness.

The Right Response To
The Wilderness
· · · · · · · · · · · · · · · · ·

Your response to the wilderness will determine how long you stay in the wilderness. Unfortunately, the dangers of the wilderness can cause a person to become disoriented and confused. The result is that people get stuck in this dry, desert-like place and end up going around in circles, struggling to reach their destiny. To pass the test of the wilderness, a person must respond properly to the wilderness. The wrong response holds you in the dry place, while a right response provides the passage out. Here are three important responses that will help us pass through the wilderness in the shortest possible time:

1 **Keep an attitude of gratitude.**
Don't complain about what you don't have, but focus on what you do have. The wilderness has a way of distorting the facts and showing you an inaccurate perspective. Even in dry times, there are plenty of things to be thankful for. The Apostle Paul knew what being in the wilderness meant. Over the course of his ministry, he was persecuted, beaten, and imprisoned, yet in one of his letters, he writes, ". . . give thanks in all circumstances, for this is God's will for you in Christ Jesus," (1 Thessalonians 5:18, NIV). In all circumstances. Maintain your attitude of gratitude.

2 Don't fix the blame. Fix the problem.

So many people fall into the blame game. When someone experiences a problem, the blame game means they blame their parents, their boss, the government, their neighbor, or whoever they can. Even if someone contributed to your burden, don't waste your energy on placing blame. Put your energy into fixing the problem.

3 Don't look back.

Life has no rewind button. Replaying yesterday means losing today. Reflecting on the "good old days" has caused many to miss out on today's possibilities. The Bible even says: "Don't long for 'the good old days.' This is not wise," (Ecclesiastes 7:10, NLT). Instead, fix your focus forward to the other side of the wilderness: "No, dear brothers and sisters, I have not achieved it, but I focus on this one thing: Forgetting the past and looking forward to what lies ahead, I press on to reach the end of the race and receive the heavenly prize for which God, through Christ Jesus, is calling us," (Philippians 3:13–14, NLT).

Conquering Containment

The strategy of evil is to contain good, to keep people from growing and prospering, to keep every good work from increasing. If you dream of improving your lifestyle or improving the world, you've entered a battle against containment. The three areas we must constantly oppose containment in are our lifestyle, our community, and our church.

I'm told that if you put fleas in a jar[4] with a lid on it, they jump up repeatedly, hitting their heads on the lid as they try to get out. After repeated bumps on the head, however, they learn their limitations. The fleas start not jumping high enough to hit the lid. This is where you can literally take the lid off, and they will stay in the jar completely unaware that the lid is no longer containing them. This is true for us in the wilderness where a "lid" has a way of conditioning us to stay within fixed boundaries.

We can allow too many bumps from past experiences cause us to lose our enthusiasm for life. We don't realize that the lid was only temporary. The lid was only there for a season. Consider if you're living with a lid over your life that isn't there anymore. Now the lid is off, and God has great possibilities for you.

In Genesis 30, you'll find the story of two men: Laban and Jacob. Jacob worked hard and wanted to prosper. Laban did everything he could to contain his nephew Jacob and to see his dreams denied. There are two powerful messages in this story. One is that delayed is not denied, and the other is that man cannot stop God's blessing.

Just because your dream of better things has not happened yet, don't give up. A dream delayed is not necessarily a dream denied. Jacob thought it would happen sooner, but he stayed on course pursuing his dream for twenty years. Eventually, everything he had worked for was achieved. Although Laban cheated him and changed his wages ten times, Jacob's hard work and

perseverance brought him great wealth and blessings. Be encouraged by this story. Man cannot stop God's blessing from coming into your life. When we do the things required to prosper, by God's principles, nothing can hinder our eventual blessing.

Avoiding The Wilderness Routine

One strong characteristic of the wilderness is that of a routine lifestyle. Remember, the object is to pass the test and move on. The wilderness is not where you want to stay. The problem with tolerating the status quo is that it lulls you into complacency. Once we have tolerated wilderness ways and habits long enough, it gets easier to accept them as a permanent way of life. We accept that it will never get better, but by accepting it, we then establish it. Many people have fallen into routine marriage habits. Others have become what I call "routine Christians." It's easy for routine to take over in the wilderness, causing us to enter a cycle of repetitive action that is getting us nowhere new. Not much changes and nothing gets better in the routine mode. Routine Christianity is a lifestyle that is lacking Christ-like progress or vision. This condition is marked by an increasing void of joy and satisfaction. Complaining becomes normal, everyday conversation when a person is in the cycle of routine Christianity.

Seven Symptoms of
R.O.U.T.I.N.E. Christianity

R = Rut

O = Obstinate State Of Mind

U = Unbelief

T = Tradition

I = Ignorance

N = Nature Of The Flesh

E = Emptiness of Spirit

Life was not meant to be routine. Life was meant to be progressive, new, adventurous, and full. Jesus said it Himself that, "I have come that they may have life, and have it to the full," (John 10:10, NIV).

Breaking out of the wilderness can cause you to step into a deeper level of trust and faith as well as a new level of abundance. The wilderness cannot hold you after you make the proper adjustments. David looked back at the testing of his ancestors and rejoiced at the final outcome of abundance.

In one of his Psalms, he wrote, "For you, O God, tested us; you refine us like silver. You brought us into prison and laid burdens on our backs. You let men ride over our heads; we went through fire and water, but you brought us to a place of abundance," (Psalm 66:10–12, NIV). In a similar way, the test of the wilderness is designed for a better end, not a bitter one. What is it we need to break out of? Let's revisit again, the seven symptoms of R.O.U.T.I.N.E. Christianity, with a breakout in mind.

The Rut

. . . .

When was the last time you did something for the first time? Many people today live in a state of boredom as if it's the only place on earth. Boring people live there. They have boring jobs, boring homes, boring marriages, and they attend boring churches. The truth, however, is that it's not the job, home, marriage or church—it's the person who is boring. If your life is boring, talk to the person in the mirror tomorrow morning and tell them to "get a life." Decide today to leave the rut of boredom.

Likewise, don't confuse activity with accomplishment. Just because the wheels are spinning and some mud is flying, doesn't mean you're going somewhere. Unless you're moving, the scenery stays the same, and that scenery is less than exciting. Accomplishment, on the other hand, will bring forward motion and the discovery of new territory. We live in a fast-paced society where people are busier than they've ever been. Go ahead and ask your coworker or friend how they're doing, and I bet they respond with "busy." Busy can be boring unless you're making progress.

Obstinate State Of Mind

The place of promise is just beyond your wilderness experience. Don't get stuck in a state of mind that resists changes in yourself. Keep learning and growing yourself to the next level. There are attitudes to adjust, like how sails adjust to winds, which will move you forward to new things. Don't grow sentimentally attached to your past like the Israelites did. Have faith that God has something better on the other side of the wilderness. Make room for the new by releasing the old. Let it go.

Unbelief

Recently, I went in for a physical exam. The doctors hooked me up to a monitor and put me on a treadmill. They continued to increase the speed, pushing me to my maximum potential. They were testing the strength of my heart, because the only way to know the heart's strength is to put it under pressure and watch how it performs. In that same way, faith is not known until it is tested by difficult circumstances. The wilderness reveals unbelief if you stop anticipating God's fulfillment of His promises. Unbelief keeps people in routine and out of the Promised Land. Fight unbelief with declarations of faith. Identify God's promise for your future and write it down. Say it. Repeat it. Keep saying it out loud until you believe it.

Tradition
. . . .

Tradition has held people in dry places. It causes misplaced loyalty, resulting in an obligation and allegiance to the wrong people or things. Tradition can be good when it is providing progress and growth. When it begins to hinder our journey toward our Promised Land, it must be evaluated. Be quick to change unproductive methods and locate a new and productive one.

For Christian leaders, it's important not to confuse methods with the message. The message is sacred, but the methods are not. The Gospel message will adapt well to different cultures and can be packaged for different ages, ethnicities, political backgrounds, and genders. Some people struggle with different music and message styles. These things are only methods and should change and adapt to various groups of people, and these methods should change with the surroundings in order to relate to people. For example, 20 years ago it was unheard of for a pastor to get on the platform in jeans and Jordans. Now it's common. The message is the same, but it's packaged in the method of relevance. Keep your allegiance to the spreading of the Gospel message and avoid getting hung up or stuck on traditional methods.

Ignorance
. . . .

The routine may continue until your knowledge increases enough to take you into a new place. People often say "the truth will set you free" thinking that they are quoting scripture. In actuality, that quotation is incomplete. The Scripture in its entirety says, "You shall know the truth and the truth will set you free," (John 8:32, NIV). It's not the presence of truth that will deliver you from the wilderness, but the knowledge of truth. Say to yourself, "The truth cannot help me, unless I know it." As you say this, you're beginning to realize how ignorance can stop you and hold you in an unwanted routine.

God even told the prophet Hosea, ". . . my people are destroyed from lack of knowledge," (Hosea 4:6, NIV). Take a look at the differences between knowledge, understanding and wisdom:

- Knowledge is the gathering of information.
- Understanding is the interpretation of information.
- Wisdom is the application of information.

Know the truth, seek to understand it, and then apply it to your life.

The Nature Of The Flesh

Grumbling, complaining, and accusing were all hindering the dream of the Promised Land from becoming reality for the children of Israel. What about you? What's one thing you are doing that is hindering your progress? You may have thought of it as family tradition and accepted it as a harmless mannerism. If it's hindering you, it's not harmless. In 1 Peter, we are encouraged to rethink our habits when Peter writes, "Dear friends, I urge you as strangers and exiles to abstain from sinful desires that wage war against the soul.," (1 Peter 2:11, CSB). Begin now to ask God to help you break the gravity-like pull of unwanted negative habits that hold you back from your full potential. The ways of the flesh war against the wellness of your soul.

Emptiness Of Spirit

Just as the desert lacks the resources to provide life and vitality, a dry spirit lacks the ability to provide those things that bring personal growth. Your spirit holds the fuel of life, and when it's empty, you find yourself in a drained, weary condition. A lack of inspiration will make it impossible to journey on to your destination. You can keep the life of God flowing into your spirit with singing, praising, reading, hearing, and proclaiming God's Word in your life. Three habits for spiritual health are found in Ephesians 5:18:

1 **I should *"speak to others in psalms, hymns, and spiritual songs."***

This can only happen in church services, prayer meetings, and places where believers impact faith to one another through our words and songs. Please don't go around your office trying to sing worship songs to win people over to Christ, but build yourself up and fill your spirit by getting planted in a local church and attending regularly.

2 **I should sing and *"make music in my heart."***

Notice the encouragement to make the music. Create a song within. Music is powerful. What songs do you have in your head? Why not take time to get some positive messages in your heart through music? There is plenty of positive music out there including great worship albums with quality lyrics to encourage you.

3 **I should always *"give thanks to God for everything."***

When we express appreciation for life's blessings, our spirits are refreshed and lifted. You've more than likely heard the phrase "find the silver lining." This I could argue is the Christian version: No matter what we face, if we look hard enough, we can find something to thank God for in a situation. If you're at a loss for something, start with being thankful that you still have breath in your lungs.

Change Is The Constant
Companion Of Progress
. . . .

When in the wilderness, it's important to stay open to change in your life. We cannot have progress without change. Not all change leads to progress, but all progress requires change. Sometimes people sincerely want progress, but they don't want to accept change. Picture in your mind progress holding hands with change. What happens is that people call for progress to come into their life. They pray for progress. But as progress approaches, they begin to see the changes attached and then refuse both progress and change. To reach your full potential in life, you must make friends with change. Start seeing change as a positive thing and welcome it into your life. None of us would feel right about a son or daughter who was still in diapers at the age of six. We want to see progress, and with that, comes change. When God gets ready to take us to a new level in life, we have to accept change.

A common error people make when God is leading them to higher ground is to avoid making the crucial and proper changes. They sense God drawing them to greater things, but they substitute wrong changes for right ones. The wrong changes are simply changes that do not bring maturity and growth. For example, when it's time to lose weight, it's important to know what to stop eating and what to start eating. If you just change from fried fish to fried potatoes, you won't lose weight. You made a change,

Not all change leads to progress, but all **progress requires change.**

but you didn't make the right one.

The people of Israel tried to change everything else except their wrong attitudes. They blamed the leaders, one another, God, and anything else they could think of for their lack of progress. Many people get in the wilderness and think, "I must change my church, my job, my spouse, my clothes, etc." Usually, they try to change everything other than the thing God is wanting them to change. Single people think the answer is being married, and some married people think the answer is being single again. Leaders blame followers, and followers blame leaders. The government blames the people, and the people blame the government. The key to proper change begins within us. This kind of change brings progress along with it.

Faith For The Future

One last thing to note about the wilderness—when you are in the wilderness, you will always feel a strong temptation to go back to the past, rather than having faith for the future. The prophet Isaiah wrote, "Forget the former things; do not dwell on the past. See, I am doing a new thing! Now it springs up; do you not perceive it? I am making a way in the desert and streams in the wasteland," (Isaiah 43: 18–19, NIV). Life has no rewind button. What was, is not what should be, if you are living a life of progress. Your children are growing. Your body is changing. People around you may come and go—but God is with you today and will be with you tomorrow. Have faith for the future!

Think-it-Out

. . . .

☐ Describe a time where you were in the wilderness and how you handled it. What would you do differently now that you've read this chapter?

....

☐ Have you ever placed lids on your potential? What are some things you can do today to push past it?

....

☐ What does having faith for the future look like in your specific situation?

....

☐ Identify three of God's promises for your future and write them down.

....

....

....

....

....

Live-it-Out

. . . .

☐ What changes can you make today to see progress happen in your life?

....

☐ How are you going to let go of some of the past to make room for what God is trying to do right now?

....

☐ This week, write out a declaration of faith each morning. This could be in a journal or on a post-it note on your bathroom mirror. (Examples: "God has a good plan for my future." or "I am deeply loved by my heavenly Father.")

....

☐ Memorize 1 Thessalonians 5:16–18 and apply its words to your situation right now.

Rejoice always, pray continually, give thanks in all circumstances, for this is God's will for you in Christ Jesus . . .

1 Thessalonians 5:18

5
The Authority
Test

**THIS TEST COMES TO PROVE YOUR
RESPECT FOR THE AUTHORITY
THAT GOD HAS PUT IN YOUR LIFE.**

The Question: Do You Respect And Appreciate The Authority God Has Put In Your Life?

. . . .

Then He said to them, "Therefore render to Caesar the things that are Caesar's, and to God the things that are God's."

Matthew 22:21, ESV

In every worthwhile endeavor of society, there is a genuine need for an authority structure. What authority actually looks like is dependant on the system that needs it. In some instances, authority may look like a chain of command or an organizational chart. In others, there may be a group of leaders who make decisions together. However we define it or whatever we call it, God's intention for authority is for it to be the solution to chaos, lawlessness, and poor organization. Healthy authority accomplishes that goal. From principals to presidents, from parents to media personalities, examples of the effects of healthy authority are everywhere. Unfortunately, there are also examples of authority gone wrong—and the results can be disastrous.

Jesus was no stranger to the concept of authority. As a part of a Jewish family living in a territory of the Roman empire, Jesus understood the importance and complexity of authority—both good and bad. In Matthew 22, Jesus provides a great example of how to think about authority. A group of Pharisees and Herodians, hoping to get Jesus to say something controversial, ask Him whether or not they should pay a tax to Caesar. For Jesus to say that they should pay the tax would be seen as dishonoring to His own religion and heritage, but if He were to say that they should not pay the tax that would make Him a revolutionary in the eyes of Rome.

Instead of offering them the yes-or-no answer they were looking for, Jesus reveals that our response to authority—particularly to corrupt authority—is one that defies our natural response. Jesus told them, "Therefore render to Caesar the things that are Caesar's, and to God the things that are God's," (Luke 20:25, ESV). This answer shows how we can, in most cases, pass the Authority Test that maintains respect for those in authority. If Caesar asks for a coin, give him a coin. After all, his face was on it! But Caesar also wanted the *worship* of his subjects and, as Jesus said, our worship should only belong to God.

Developing A Proper Attitude Toward Authority

The Authority Test will always reveal our attitudes toward the authority figures in our lives. If we struggle with those people telling us what to do, this test will reveal it. If we resent those over us, this test will reveal it. If we despise those in authority having privileges that we don't have, this test will reveal it. To pass the test, we must focus our attention not on the errors of those in authority, but on our attitude toward authority. More often than not, when we want to change or challenge authority, God is wanting to change or challenge our attitude toward authority.

Our greatest test involving authority comes when we disagree with authority. As long as our authorities do everything like we want them to, there can be no testing of our respect for authority. This means that we must observe our attitude most when we don't understand or agree with the decisions and actions of those in authority. I can almost hear the outcry against what I just wrote: "But what about bad authority or corrupt leadership? Are you telling me I have to submit myself to authority even when authority is wrong?"

My hope is to answer some of these questions in this chapter. However, I must remind you that there have always been "bad" or "corrupt" authorities, and there always will be. Every single person will have unfortunate encounters with authority figures who are abusing and misusing their power. When this happens, our goal is to develop a good attitude toward authority that is not changed by people in authority whether good or bad. Here's three things that can help us develop a good attitude toward authority.

1 AN AWARENESS OF AUTHORITY

A good attitude toward authority begins with an

Our greatest test involving authority comes when we disagree with authority.

awareness of authority. When asked about paying the tax, Jesus acknowledged Caesar's position and his own responsibility to honor that position. Locate those in positions of authority in your life. Have you accepted them as authorities? Do you admit that they have positions, which place them in authority? Do you find yourself reluctant and trying to be "equal" with them? Only when we are willing to acknowledge positions of authority that exist in our lives can we move forward into the place of accepting and respecting their authority.

Did Jesus honor Caesar because of who Caesar was as a person? Probably not. He honored Caesar, because He had an awareness of Caesar's position of authority. Let me help you consider some areas where authority should exist in your life:

1   In your family
2   In your career/job
3   At your church
4   At your school
5   In your community
6   In the government of your nation

As you consider these areas where authority should exist, take note of your attitude. Is it difficult to acknowledge authority in these cases? We can improve attitudes toward authority only after we locate and accept authority.

2 TO EXPERIENCE WHAT IT'S LIKE TO BE IN AND UNDER AUTHORITY

Jesus' famous encounter with the Pharisees about Caesar's tax wasn't the only time we see His understanding of authority in action. In Luke, Jesus meets a Roman centurion who makes a lasting impression on Him. The centurion tells Jesus, "For I myself am a man under authority, with soldiers under me. I tell this one, 'Go,' and he goes; and that one, 'Come,' and he comes. I say to my servant, 'Do this,' and he does it . . ." (Luke 7:8, NIV).

The centurion is assuring Jesus that he understands if Jesus cannot personally come to pray for the sick servant. He is saying, "I know about delegating others to handle responsibilities when you have many who need you." As a pastor, I sometimes wish that all of our congregation realized that one pastor cannot and should not do all the works of ministry in a church. There are people who have unrealistic and downright crazy expectations of the life of a pastor. Their idea can look something like this:

He preaches exactly 20 minutes and then sits down. He condemns sin, but never hurts anyone's feelings. He works from 8:00AM to 10:00PM in every type of work, from preaching to taxi service. He makes 60 dollars a week, wears good clothes, buys good books regularly, has a nice family, drives a good car, and gives 30 dollars a week to the church. He also stands ready to contribute to every good work that comes along. He is 26-years-old and has been preaching 30 years. He is tall and short, thin and heavyset, plain-looking and handsome. He has one brown eye and one blue, hair parted in the middle, left side straight and dark, the other side wavy and blonde. He has a burning desire to work with teenagers and spends all his time with the older folks. He smiles all the time with a straight face, because he has a sense of humor that keeps him seriously dedicated to his work. He makes 15 calls a day to church members, spends all his time evangelizing the unchurched, and is never out of his office.

He is truly a remarkable person ... and he does not exist.

That's right, that guy doesn't exist. Now, back to the point. The centurion's respect and experience for authority caused him to say, "It's okay, Jesus, if You can't come. If You can just speak the word or send someone, I know my servant will be healed." I have found it helpful to experience both sides of authority. Only when you can say, "I know what it's like to be in and under authority," can you genuinely appreciate the blessings of authority. Only when you've been in authority can you relate to those in authority. I find that someone who has been in responsible places of authority, generally will be less critical of others who are doing their best in responsible positions of authority.

As a kid, I often questioned my parent's actions and decisions, but I have found that the older I get, the smarter I realize they were. It's easier to understand once you are where they were. Only after having our own children and assuming responsibility for them, do we understand why our parents did what they did. Until you are a manager, you won't fully appreciate the skills of management. Until you oversee others, you'll never understand the challenge of doing so. Until you lead or govern, you'll have a limited perspective of what it's like to be in authority. Likewise, if and when you are in authority, don't forget what it's like to be under authority. The best leaders use the experiences they had while under authority to help them be better while in authority.

3 TO ACCEPT GOD'S WORD CONCERNING AUTHORITY

It's important for us to remember that the Bible was written by and about people who had the same kind of experiences with authority as we do. They all had the opportunity to deal with crooked governments, bad parents, lazy bosses, and unjust religious leaders. Even with all of that being true, the Bible is absolute in its command that we accept and honor authority. Let's look at a few key Scriptures:

- "Every person is to be in subjection to the governing authorities. For there is no authority except from God, and those which exist are established by God," (Romans 13:1, NASB).
- "Wives, submit to your husbands, as is fitting in the Lord. Husbands, love your wives and do not be harsh with them. Children, obey your parents in everything, for this pleases the Lord. Fathers, do not embitter your children, or they will become

discouraged. Slaves, obey your earthly masters in everything, and do it, not only when their eye is on you and to win their favor, but with sincerity of heart and reverence for the Lord," (Colossians 3:18–22, NIV).

· "Obey your leaders and submit to them, for they are keeping watch over your souls, as those who will have to give an account. Let them do this with joy and not with groaning, for that would be of no advantage to you," (Hebrews 13:17, ESV).

The following are Bible words, which describe a good attitude toward authority:

· *Submission*—surrendering, obedience, resignation "Every person is to be in subjection to the governing authorities . . ." (Romans 13:1, NASB).

· *Respect*—to show consideration, honor or esteem for ". . . should consider their masters worthy of full respect . . ." (1 Timothy 6:1, NIV).

· *Obey*—to carry out orders, to be guided by Obey those who rule over you . . ." (Hebrews 13:7, KJV).

· *Honor*—to respect greatly, to show high regard for "Give to everyone what you owe them . . . if respect, then respect; if honor, then honor," (Romans 13:7, NIV).

Below are Bible words, which describe a wrong attitude toward authority:

- *Rebellion*—a defiance or opposition to authority "For rebellion is like the sin of divination . . ." (1 Samuel 15:23, NIV).
- *Sedition*—the stirring up of discontent, resistance, or rebellion against the government or authority in power
  "Now the works of the flesh are manifest, which are these . . . seditions . . ." (Galatians 5:19–21, KJV).
- *Railer*—one who speaks bitterly with complaint, aimed at or against something or someone
  "Do not keep company, if any man that is called a brother be a railer . . ." (1 Corinthians 5:11, KJV).
- *Insurrection*—a rising up against established authority, inclined to be less visible in nation than rebellion
  "Hide me from the secret council of the wicked; from the insurrection of the workers of iniquity," (Psalm 64:2, KJV).

Recognizing Legitimate Authority

1 LEGITIMATE AUTHORITY IS BASED ON THE BALANCING OF PRIVILEGE WITH RESPONSIBILITY.

This revelation is especially important to all who reach for "equality" and resist the leadership of others. Let me explain this with the following examples:

Example A:

If you have two daughters, one 15 and the other 5, the 15-year-old should have responsibilities that your 5-year-old doesn't have. She should also have privileges that the 5-year-old doesn't have. If they are home alone, a natural authority should kick in. As a parent, you should be able to expect the 15-year-old to be responsible for the safety and care of the 5-year-old. However, unless the 15-year-old also has some privileges of authority, she should not be held responsible.

Unless you can tell the 5-year-old, "Your sister is in charge. Listen to her and obey her," it would not be fair to hold the older sister responsible when the 5-year-old didn't clean her room, put away toys, or go to bed on time. If the 15-year-old is ultimately held responsible, she needs the privilege of making the decisions in the house that evening.

Example B:

In business organizations, the owner is responsible for the profits and losses. If you work for a company that can't pay its bills, the collectors don't come to you, they go to the owners. Owners sign documents and legal papers that name them as the individual responsible for the company. Often owners invest everything they have in starting a company. So, it's only fair that they have the privilege of decision making. It's their privilege not to do what an employee may want them to do. It doesn't make them an abusive authority if they make demands on employees without accepting their demands in return. That's their privilege. It's not inappropriate and should not cause offense. It's the privilege that comes with responsibility.

In Numbers 12, Miriam and Aaron sought the privileges of Moses when they had not been given the responsibilities of Moses. God's response was heated, to say the least. He went to a great length to explain to them that they were not in an equal place of responsibility, and therefore, they did not have the privilege of speaking as Moses spoke.

A few times in my ministry, especially when our church was smaller, somebody would come along and want me to give them speaking privileges in our church. They seemed to feel that since they were attending our church, if they claimed to be called to ministry, I should let them speak in our services. I've heard the same sound that Miriam and Aaron made on more than one occasion, "What makes you so special that you should speak all the time? I'm also called into ministry and should be heard." What these people did not understand was that I was not selfishly hoarding the pulpit at our church. I had been given responsibility to lead and feed the church. I must answer to God for the ministry to the people. Along with that responsibility, was the privilege to be the consistent and clear voice to the people. God made me responsible to minister to the needs of the people and the decision of who should speak was my privilege to choose. Legitimate authority is not responsibility without privilege. Nor is it privilege without responsibility.

2 LEGITIMATE AUTHORITY IS FUNCTIONAL AUTHORITY.

Without structures of authority, our homes, work-places, communities, churches, and nations would be ruled by chaos. This is why legitimate authority always has a functional purpose. When there is authority, just for the sake of authority, it quickly becomes a dictatorship driven by power rather than purpose. It exists to flex its muscles and exercise power over others. Functional authority exists to accomplish a purpose and to move the group in a healthy direction. It can be short term or long term, but once the purpose is accomplished, the authority ceases to exist.

Examples of functional authority:

A   A flight attendant on an airplane is giving instructions to sit down and fasten your seat belt. That authority is necessary for safety while on board the plane. Once you exit the airplane, the flight attendant's authority ceases to have a functional purpose.

B   A teacher in a classroom is telling our children how to behave. That authority is necessary for the students to learn. When school is over, the teacher's authority no longer has a functional purpose.

C   A police officer is ticketing a speeding motorist. That authority exists to keep the streets safe and vehicles at a reasonable speed. If an officer exercises authority outside that functional purpose, their authority ceases to be legitimate.

3 LEGITIMATE AUTHORITY IS DELEGATED AUTHORITY.

Authority does not cease to be legitimate simply because it is received from a higher authority.

- A manager's authority is usually received from an owner or higher authority.
- Parents may delegate authority to a babysitter.
- A pastor may delegate authority to other pastors and leaders.

Jesus acknowledged Pilate's God-given authority as legitimate, even though it would not work in His interest. In John, it says, "Jesus answered, 'You would have no power over Me if it were not given to you from above,'" (John 19:11, NIV). He is not denying Pilate's authority. He is acknowledging it as God-given or God-delegated authority.

For those who are in positions of delegated authority, remember that delegated authority should always represent the best interest of those in higher authority. Delegated authority should guard against seeking its own interest when in conflict with those over them. People who don't work as hard when their boss is not around are not seeking the best interest of the company they work for.

Whatever level you're at in an authority structure,

recognize your need to fulfill the goals of those you work for. A baseball team has several coaches and one manager. The pitching coach, batting coach, and third base coach should all adapt their coaching to the strategies and approach of the manager. Some managers want to play fast-paced, risky baseball. The coaches should pass that philosophy on to the players. The coach, as a delegated authority, should coach according to the manager's philosophy at all times. If he has a differing strategy than the manager, the players must never hear it. He is a delegated authority whose role is to be an extension of a higher authority. His authority is legitimate and should serve the interest of a higher authority.

For those who delegate, remember that although delegating is the passing on of responsibilities, delegation never relieves you of responsibilities. Because you delegate something, does not mean you are no longer responsible for it being accomplished. Often young managers or leaders will try to excuse failure by saying to a higher authority, "I gave it to so and so to do, and they didn't do it," as if to say, "It's not my fault. Don't blame me." Those who accept responsibility eventually have more responsibilities, while those who avoid responsibility eventually have less responsibility. Jesus said, "If you want to be great, learn to serve." In other words, accept responsibility. Those who accept responsibility will grow in greatness.

Passing The Authority Test

· ·

Unfortunately, there are instances of legitimate authority behaving in ways that are inappropriate, inconsiderate, and inexcusable. Over the past few years, news headlines seemed to be flooded with examples of people who are in authority doing and saying things that cause outrage on a massive scale. The unfortunate side-effect of this is that our culture tends to generalize a group of people because of the actions of one person. But we all know from our own experiences that this isn't a fair way to behave.

As Christians, we sometimes see others who claim to share our faith using tactics that violate our understanding of God's love for everyone. The same is true for a police officer who unfairly treats a civilian based on their race. Yes, the officer is wrong, but the example of that one officer doesn't mean that all police officers are bad. A business leader might be exposed as being corrupt. He or she should have to pay the punishment, but we have to fight against the temptation to assume that every other business leader is the same. One example of corporate corruption doesn't make the whole corporate world corrupt.

It is vitally important for us, as Christians, to remember that when authority fails, God is looking at our response. In telling the Pharisees to pay the tax to Caesar—who demanded the worship of his subjects—Jesus showed that He maintained an accurate attitude towards authority that has become corrupt. In that case, it wasn't about the person. It was about honoring what God had allowed to be in place. When that authority fails, it is *our* attitude that will be revealed. The failure may be:

· A wrong decision by someone in authority
· A moral failure by someone in authority
· Immature actions by someone in authority
· Unfair treatment by someone in authority
· Discrimination by someone in authority

All of these are obvious failures of integrity, wisdom, character, and maturity. However, in Biblical examples of failed authority, God still focused His attention on the reactions of those under that authority. He repeatedly let it serve as a time of testing, closely observing their response to the failed authority.

For example, in Genesis 9, although Noah's conduct was wrong, his failure became a test for his sons. Both obedience and rebellion were revealed. And again in I Samuel, King Saul was in authority, but he was wrong. And, still David said, "Who can touch the Lord's anointed and be guiltless?" (1 Samuel 26:9, NIV). Thus proving to God his ability to grow in character, not in criticism, when dealing with a failed authority.

It's important to focus on what God wants us to learn when we see the errors of those in authority. The ability to respond properly and without rebellion is the purpose of the test. There is always a right response to

There is always a right response to wrong authority.

wrong authority. When authority makes demands on you that are in violation of your conscience, there is a right response. When authority is abusive toward you, there is a right response. When authority extends beyond its functional purpose, there is a right response. The right response can never include a physical or verbal attack on authority. The right response can never include a demonstration of anger or hostility. The right response can never be to stir up strife against authority by railing on authority to others. The most common right responses to wrong authority are simple and few. Let me give you two:

1 APPEAL TO A HIGHER AUTHORITY.

Since most authority is delegated, there is usually someone else we can turn to when we feel like there is corrupt authority. This doesn't mean that we have the opportunity to gossip or complain to our boss's boss when we don't get our way. When there is someone who is abusing their power and exploiting people, however, prayerfully bringing awareness to a higher authority is permissible. Ultimately, the highest authority we can turn to is God. So when all else fails (and hopefully before!) pray about how to handle your situation, pray for the person in authority, and pray for God to move in the hearts of everyone involved.

2 PEACEFUL WITHDRAWAL FROM THE AUTHORITY'S JURISDICTION OR SPHERE OF POWER.

When Saul persecuted David to the point of literally throwing spears at him, David provided us with an incredible example for how to remove yourself from the rule of an unjust and dangerous authority. When David escaped from Saul, he didn't spread the word, he didn't raise up an army, he didn't take anyone with him. Even though he was blameless, David refused to invite anyone else into his offense. He knew that doing so would require slandering his authority whom he called, "The Lord's anointed."

Because David maintained an attitude of honor while in exile from a corrupt leader, God blessed him with an army of loyal followers. And, eventually, God kept His word and made David the anointed King of the Israelites.

A member of the Special Forces showed me recently their motto and mission statement. It's a picture of intersecting daggers representing the V-42 dagger issued to each member of the Force. The encircling scroll bears the Special Forces motto, De Oppresso Liber, which is translated from Latin as "To free the oppressed." As I looked at the motto, I was reminded that there are times in history when evil leaders have become dictators over innocent people, and I'm proud to be a citizen in a nation that has a mission to free the oppressed. Those extreme situations are very different, and different rules would apply. Having said that, never assume that those severe and extreme circumstances negate the need for us to live a life of honor towards the authority's God has placed over us. Everything's better with honor. Our homes are better with honor. Our schools are better with honor. Our city is better with honor. Our church is better with honor, and our nation is better with honor.

Remember, there is always a right response even when the authority is wrong. It is usually less about who is in authority and what they are doing or saying, and more about how you are going to respond. Choose honor. And, when that has been exhausted on all sides, choose honor again.

Think-it-Out

· · · · · · · · · · · · · ·

☐ Have you ever struggled with authority? Why or why not?

....

☐ If you are in a position of authority, how would your rate your leadership on a scale of 1–10. What are some ways you can improve? (Also, rate yourself if you are under authority.)

....

☐ How can you take control of your reactions to authority?

....

☐ What does submitting to authority look like in your everyday life?

....

☐ If someone in authority over you were to take away your current role and ask you to be under another leader in a different area, how would you react? How can you use this chapter to help you?

....

☐ Knowing that God is the ultimate authority, how does that change your perspective on your current situation?

....

....

Live-it-Out
. . . .

☐ Think about some ways you can respond well to authority.

....

☐ Who is in authority over you? Think of ways that you can improve your relationship with them.

....

☐ Evaluate the people you surround yourself with and their approach to authority. Consider whether their perspectives influence your approach to authority.Memorize Romans 13:1 to help you pass the Authority Test.

Let everyone be subject to the governing authorities, for there is no authority except that which God has established. The authorities that exist have been established by God.

Romans 13:1

6
The Warfare Test

THIS TEST OCCURS WHEN YOU ARE IN THE WILL OF GOD AND ARE EXPERIENCING ADVERSITY.

The Question: What is Your Adversity Quotient?

. . . .

Jesus replied, "Do what you came for, friend."
Then the men stepped forward, seized Jesus,
and arrested Him.

Matthew 26:50, NIV

O ne of the mistakes people make is to assume that if God wants you to have something you won't have to fight for it. You won't have to plan for it, you won't have to have a vision for it and you won't have to work for it. A person can believe, "If God wants me to have something I don't have to do anything, He will just cause it to happen in my life." That thought has caused a lot of people to miss out on the blessings, opportunities, and progress that God has planned for them. Just because God has plans, places, and purpose for you doesn't mean you don't have to fight for them!

What we accomplish in life is not based on what we want, but on how much we want it and how willing we are to fight for it. One undeniable ingredient that helps to determine our personal potential, is our capacity to fight for what we want to see in our future. I like to think about it like this: "It's not the size of the dog in the fight, but the size of fight in the dog," (Mark Twain). No doubt about

What we accomplish in life is not based on what we want, **but on how much we want it.**

it, people with less talent and more fight will go further in life than the very talented person who gives up when they face adversity. At a young age, I was tremendously inspired by a speech I read about that Winston Churchill gave to the British Parliament on June 4, 1940. With his country under attack from a powerful German army, he stood boldly before his countrymen and declared:

> *"We shall go on to the end, we shall fight in France, we shall fight on the seas and oceans, we shall fight with growing strength and growing confidence in the air, we shall defend our island whatever the cost may be, we shall fight on the beaches, we shall fight on the landing grounds, we shall fight in the fields and in the streets, we shall fight in the hills; we shall never surrender . . ."*

Winston Churchill, The Finest Hour[5]

The warfare test comes into our lives to prove how well we respond to adversity. Being aware of this test will help us build our tolerance for pain and increase our endurance to keep fighting through resistance in difficult times. Each time we pass this test in the different seasons of our lives, we are developing better eyes to identify what enemies we face as well as developing a champion spirit. It may help you to know that each one of us has an overcomer in us. Maybe the fighter in you is refrained or untrained.

Maybe the fighter has been reluctant to rise up with courage to face adversity. Maybe the fight in you has laid dormant because of a huge setback or major disappointment in your life. But all of us are created with a fighter inside of us. God created us that way!

Jesus found Himself in the warfare test during His ministry and throughout His life. He faced this test especially at the end of His earthly ministry when He is in the Garden of Gethsemane praying, "not My will, but Yours be done," (Luke 22:42, NIV). There He was, right in the middle of the will of God with His own disciples falling asleep instead of praying with Him, and then Judas (a former disciple), brings a small army to arrest Him. You could look at these moments and think *why did it have to happen this way*, but everything was part of a bigger plan for Jesus. At every obstacle, He kept pressing forward understanding that life wouldn't be easy just because He was in the will of God. Instead, He was aware that He could and would experience problems along the journey. He showed us what it looks like to have a high tolerance for adversity. It happened this way so that Jesus could model how to handle adversity for us.

The Heart Of A Champion

The fight for your future is more internal than external. The greatest enemy of your future is not what happens, but it's how you see yourself when it happens. When you lose a job or have a financial setback or a relationship gone wrong or a personal failure—it's not that thing that defines you. It's how you see yourself. It's how you respond. A lot of people assume that if God's will includes a certain pathway that they will not have to fight battles along the way because they are "in God's plan." That couldn't be farther from the truth. We have to fight for our future! We will fight battles externally and we will fight battles internally. We will face adversity as we advance through God's plan and purpose for our lives. And, how much we can handle comes down to our inner strength.

A person with a lot of inner strength is commonly described as having "a lot of heart." The warfare test will reveal the level of your inner strength and perseverance. When the Houston Rockets won their second consecutive NBA title, their head coach was interviewed after the victory. He had a message for those who had underestimated his team: "Don't ever underestimate the heart of a champion."[6] His message was clearly directed at all of the analysts who tend to look at things like size, speed, and talent, but overlook passion, perseverance, and the will to win. The heart of a champion begins with the choice to be a champion.

The Choice Of A Champion

Your potential to conquer will be given many opportunities to prove itself through the course of a lifetime. Champions come in all sizes, shapes, and colors. They face adversity in all its various forms. They are not the "lucky" or "trouble-free" people. Champions are the overcoming people. It's not a result of where they are born, where they go to school, or what happens to them in life. The primary ingredient in the life of a champion is the choice to be a champion.

1 THE CHOICE TO BE A CHAMPION IS AN ACCEPTANCE OF GOD'S WORD, WHICH SAYS YOU ARE A CHAMPION.

Putting yourself down doesn't lift God up. If you are a Christ-follower, your life purpose at the 30,000 feet view is to glorify God with your life. Live to honor Him. That doesn't happen by putting yourself down. You shrinking doesn't make God bigger. Hiding your light doesn't make God's light brighter. The Psalmist says, "The Lord is my helper... the strength of my life... " AND the Psalmist says, "I can run through a troop and leap over a wall." In other words, believe in yourself *and* God! Have confidence in yourself that is based on your confidence in God.

The choice to be a champion lacks credibility if it is based on always feeling like a champion. I don't always feel like a champion or behave like a champion. My choice to be a champion is not a result of my earning the title of a champion, based on what I have done or what I can do. The Bible encourages us to be winners, and here are a couple of examples:

- "... in all these things we are more than conquerors through Him who loved us," (Romans 8:37, NIV).
- " ... for everyone born of God overcomes the world. This is the victory that has overcome the world, even our faith," (1 John 5:4, NIV).

Yes, we may lose battles because we are human, but according to God's Word, a Christ-follower cannot lose the war. We are destined to win! People who hesitate in making a choice to be a champion are people who are looking at their own weakness. They see all of their failures, but champions accept God's Word that declares us forgiven, justified (think of this word as "just as if I'd never sinned"), and righteous before God. This acceptance of God's Word will cause us to reign in life like a champion.

2 THE CHOICE TO BE A CHAMPION EMPOWERS A PERSON WITH THE WILL TO WIN.

"To be or not to be?" that is the question . . . not just for Shakespeare's *Hamlet*, but for each and every one of us, deciding whether we are going to step into our God-given identity as a champion or not. Until the question is answered, our will to win is on hold. Ask yourself, "What do I really want to do?" Now ask yourself, "Have I really decided to do it against all odds and whatever it takes?" This could be anything from losing weight to succeeding in business.

When you decide and make a definite choice to do

The more definite

your direction is, the greater your willpower.

something, the will to accomplish it is given direction. Our will is a powerful force waiting to receive direction. The more definite your direction is, the greater your willpower. An undecided person cannot tap into the strength of his or her will. For example, some people are not sure if they are able to serve God or not. They say they want to, but are not sure that they can. The question is not, "Can I do it?" The question is "Have I decided to do it?" A man named Joshua in the Bible decided and made an announcement to the nation of people he was leading:

> *But if serving the Lord seems undesirable to you,*
> *then choose for yourselves this day whom you will*
> *serve, whether the gods your forefathers served*
> *beyond the river, or the gods of the Amorites, in*
> *whose land you are living. But as for me and my*
> *household, we will serve the Lord.*

Joshua 24:15, NIV

Many couples have not decided yet to have a happy marriage. The question is not, "Can we do it?" The question is "Have we decided to do it?" Others have not decided to break the cycle of poverty in their life. The question is not, "Can I do it?" The question is, "Have I decided to do it?"

We all have something we want to be a champion over. We lack willpower, however, until we make the choice to be a champion. Once we make the decision, then our

Comfort is way overrated and **commit-ment is way underrated.**

will to win can begin to move us toward our goal. That choice fuels our perseverance so that we can accomplish that goal. That choice challenges us to take action. You are not fighting by *knowing* what to do. Fighting is *doing*. Doing is fighting. Are there things you know to do that you've put off doing and now you're stuck where you are? Are you that person on the border of something better that has avoided taking the next steps forward?

Comfort is way overrated and commitment is way underrated. The best things in life don't happen by being comfortable. The best things in life come from commitment. Your future and your family's future is being shaped right now by what you decide to do or not do about God's call on your life. You're not fighting for your future by knowing what to do. You're not fighting for your future by thinking about what you want to do. You fight by doing! You fight by making an all in commitment to God's plan and purpose for your life. You fight by leaving the gray zone and declaring yourself to be the champion that God created you to be.

Becoming A Champion Fighter

Some things are not necessary to become a champion fighter. Your formal education, family background, nationality, or hair color—none of those things are deal breakers. However, after you make the choice to be a champion, there are two essential fundamentals to becoming a champion fighter: the ability to take a punch and the ability to throw a punch.

Anyone who has watched professional boxing has, no doubt, seen winners whose faces were disfigured from the punishment dished out on them by their opponent. Between rounds, he goes to his corner and they work on his swollen eyes, bleeding nose, and busted lip. Then, the bell rings and he's back on his feet and into the fight. The ability to take a punch is necessary to being a champion fighter (anyone can learn this!).

When you are able to "take a punch" that means you are able to continue fighting after you get hit and even after you get knocked down. You get back up, take your position again, and keep fighting. Everyone who "steps into the ring" of God's plan, will eventually get hit hard. If you are afraid of getting hit, you can't be a champion.

Champions overcome the fear of the fight and position themselves face-to-face with the challenge. Champions have the potential to take the best their opponent can pound out and still continue to keep fighting. In 2 Corinthians, Paul writes, "We are hard pressed on every side, but not crushed; perplexed, but not in despair; persecuted, but not abandoned; struck down, but not destroyed," (2 Corinthians 4:8, NIV). This is what becoming a champion fighter is all about.

A champion has to be able to take a punch, but they also have to be more than a punching bag. They must have the ability to give a punch, to counter attack, to fight back. When the bell rings, signaling that another round is going to begin, there's no time to nurse those wounds. There's an enemy who has challenged you, taunted you, beckoned you, like the giant named Goliath asking David for a fight. You cannot turn away from it this time. You cannot ignore the challenge, there's too much at stake. It's for your family, your marriage, your future.

Fight the fight, come out swinging, kick if you have to, but whatever you do, don't stop short of feeding the carcass to the fowls of the air. Just like David, your challenger may be a giant, but this is your chance to be a champion.

The Threat Of War
. . . .

Many dreams are forsaken at the threat of war. Enemies threaten our marriage, families, and our integrity. Even God's chosen people, the Israelites, faced the threat of war while they were walking into God's promise land. After God delivered them from slavery in Egypt, we read, "If they face war, they might change their minds and return to Egypt," (Exodus 13:17, NIV).

The background on this verse is that the shortest journey to the Promised Land was through enemy territory, and God wasn't sure if they were up for the fight. So He sent them on a longer route. That's the way it is with a lot of people today. The very thought of confrontation makes them queasy with fear. They could get where God wants to take them sooner if they were willing to press forward in adversity and fight their enemy. The two most common fear responses to the enemy's threats are to ignore the enemy and hope he goes away, or to negotiate and compromise with the enemy.

The truth is, to ignore the enemy is not the same as resisting the enemy. We are encouraged as Christ-followers to "Resist the devil, and he will flee from you," (James 4:7, NIV). To simply ignore an enemy of your God-given dream is a weak response to the threat of war. On the other hand, resistance of the enemy is an active strategy of war that refuses to surrender territory. For example, in the fight of good against evil, we can refuse to give our attention to something that we sense is either a planned distraction or is plainly unworthy of our attention. This strategic resistance is a legitimate strategy of war but should not be confused with the fearful ignoring of an enemy's presence.

Another fear response to the enemy's threats is to negotiate and compromise with the enemy. Do you remember Samson in the Bible? He was a warrior of great potential and strength who got into a compromising relationship with a woman named Delilah (Judges 13–16). The fear of losing her caused him to negotiate his strength away. With the loss of his strength, he lost his vision and ultimately compromised his own destiny.

Every person who has experienced any level of success, will quickly realize that yesterday's success can become tomorrow's mediocrity. Success is an ongoing journey. The career, marriage, and the newborn baby all must have today's wisdom and skill to be healthy and strong. We congratulate people when they have a child, but real congratulations are due after they fought off all the threatening forces of evil that attempt to lay hold of the child's life and future. It's not nearly as great to have children as it is to raise them to be godly, responsible adults.

It's not a matter of *if* we will face battles that test devotion, perseverance, and character when attempting any worthwhile endeavor. It is a matter of *when*. Whether living God's way as a single person, building a business, raising children, or keeping a marriage healthy, we must not ignore or negotiate with the enemies of our potential.

Picture Your Enemy As Your Footstool

This powerful message was spoken by retiring King David as he passed the scepter of kingship to his son, Solomon, "The Lord says to my Lord: "Sit at my right hand until I make your enemies a footstool for your feet,"(Psalm 110:1, NIV).

The confidence is obvious as he speaks a prophetic command and promises the desired outcome of his enemies becoming his footstool. What a word-picture to plant in the mind of a new king! It was the picture of absolute, ongoing victory over every foe. He could see all enemies being eventually underneath his authority and power. It's impossible to pass the Warfare Test with a picture of defeat in your mind.

The pictures in our mind are powerful and self-fulfilling. These pictures are a product of our beliefs—both fear and faith. We've all heard people, after an undesirable experience say, "I knew this would happen." What we don't often realize, is that our belief that it would happen, probably contributed to it happening.

If you picture your marriage falling apart long enough, it eventually will. If you picture yourself not having enough money to enjoy life, you will fulfill that view of your future. On the other hand, people who see their marriage as happy and long-lasting will flow in the direction of that mind-picture. Likewise, people who ponder wise investments and picture a successful financial future, tend to flow in that direction and experience their desired outcome.

The Most Common Enemies
We Must Conquer

After you've lived a few years and gone through a few tests, it's easy to consider the possibility of settling in a place where God doesn't want you to settle (check out the Wilderness Test chapter for more on that). It is similar with our enemies. After we face off with our enemies enough times, we can begin to just accept them as part of the canvas of our lives. We get comfortable with allowing them access into our hearts, our minds, our physical space. When the passion fades into apathy, the enemy we face becomes like the stain in the carpet. When we first saw it, it felt like we always saw it. But, if left untreated over time, our eyes skip passed it, and its presence remains. It may become faded, but it is still there.

The most common enemies we must conquer can go unnoticed:

1 The enemies of mental, emotional, spiritual, and physical health.
2 The enemies of covenant relationships with God, family, church, and friends.
3 The enemies of prosperity.

These enemies can take many shapes and forms, but here's a few to consider:

Unbelief	Weakness
Low Self-Esteem	Sex Outside Marriage
Sickness	Selfishness
Negativity	Poor Self-Image
Bad Eating Habits	Criticism
Drugs & Alcohol Abuse	Lack of Character
Hopelessness	Lack of Integrity
Boredom	Injustice
Jealousy	Misunderstandings
Anger	Lack of Honor
Pride	Inconsistency
Lack of Consideration	Laziness
Lack of Motivation	Excessive Debt

Hoarding Attitude

Failure to Plan

Ignorance

Failure to Honor God with Tithes and Offerings

I remember reading a quote from Napoleon Hill that said, "Every adversity, every failure, every heartache carries with it the seed of an equal or greater benefit."[7] Oftentimes, our reaction to adversity limits the reach of our influence. Based on His experience in the Garden of Gethsemane, Jesus modeled passing the Warfare Test. He *knew* the hardship and torture ahead of Him, and yet He kept moving forward in the will of God, allowing it all to happen. He could have approved of one of His disciples who pulled out his sword, and responded with force, yet Jesus calmed the situation by healing the soldier in that moment (you can read about it in Luke 22). Jesus proved that we can respond to adversity with grace, perseverance, and hope. He said it Himself earlier in His ministry, and it may have been running through His mind while He was on His way to be condemned for crucifixion. He never said we wouldn't experience trouble or adversity. Instead, Jesus said, "In this world you will have trouble. But take heart! I have overcome the world," (John 16:33, NIV).

Hope is the stubborn, unrelenting determination to not allow the hardships of life to downsize the bigness of God. In the middle of a Warfare Test, it could become easy to claim victim and stay put. We all have to choose between being a victim and a victor. It's one or the other. You can't be both. I hope you choose victor.

Our reaction to adversity limits the reach of our influence.

Think-it-Out

. . . .

☐ Are you currently in the middle of the battle? If not, have you been?

....

☐ In what ways have you allowed the enemy to seem bigger than God?

....

☐ Do you try to fight your battles on your own? Why or Why not?

....

☐ Do you have a picture of victory or defeat in your mind about this season? How can you take steps to see victory?

....

☐ Look at some of the enemies listed on page 168 in this chapter and write down one or two you feel like you are facing right now.

....

....

....

....

Live-it-Out
. . . .

☐ How can you actively resist your enemies, so you don't just ignore them or begin to compromise with them?

....

☐ What steps can you take this week to win the battle against your internal and external battles?

....

☐ Gather together an "army," or community, around you in the battle you are facing. This could look like asking for prayer, serving, or seeking wisdom about what to do next.

....

☐ Commit to memory 2 Corinthians 4:8-9, and when you face adversity, this scripture will help you pass the Warfare Test.

We are hard pressed on every side, but not crushed; perplexed, but not in despair; persecuted, but not abandoned; struck down, but not destroyed.

2 Corinthians 4:8-9

7
The Offense Test

THIS TEST WILL COME TO PROVE THAT YOU ARE NOT EASILY OFFENDED AND THAT YOU HAVE THE POTENTIAL TO READILY FORGIVE OTHERS.

The Question: Are You Going To Let Circumstances And Situations In Life Offend You?

. . . .

"It is impossible that no offenses should come . . . "
—Jesus

Luke 17:1, NKJV

J esus lived an unoffended life when He had every opportunity to be offended. Think about it, He was constantly being criticized, questioned, ostracized. From the very beginning, He was born in a manger, because people wouldn't make room for Him. He could have easily allowed that to affect the way He saw His life: that He had to fight against the way people saw Him to take His place in the world. But He didn't. Instead, Jesus lived from a place of knowing who He was and not allow Himself to be defined by what man says about Him. The fact that He remained confident in who He was when others showed no respect for Him gave Him the ability to walk through extreme offense and still complete the mission in front of Him.

You may be saying to yourself right now, "Well, Pastor Kevin, I'm not Jesus, and if you knew how I was treated, what was said to me or done to me . . . you would understand that I have every right to be offended." But my goal is to help you understand that having the right to be offended doesn't lessen its consequences in your life.

For some crazy reason, we assume that holding on to an offense evens the score with the person who offended us. The truth is that when you hold on to an offense it doesn't hurt anyone else even close to how much it hurts you. Living offended is one of the most self-sabotaging decisions you can make.

Hopefully, as we move through the words of this chapter, you will recognize the power that awaits you every time you say no to offense and make the decision to push past the opportunity to be offended. Every time you pass the Offense Test is a huge win for your own life and future. Living offended is a trap while the choice to live unoffended is liberating. It sets you up to invest all your energy in the things that you can do something about. Things that are not in your past but in your future. Living unoffended means freedom of negativity and strife and freedom to invest yourself fully in the things that matter most. It doesn't mean you will no longer walk through tough time, but it means your reactions change, your focus shifts, and all your efforts are part of God's big plans for your life.

Living Offended Versus Feeling Offended

I want to encourage you to see every offense in two stages.

Stage 1 is the *feeling* of offense. This is what you feel

when offense comes. You've probably had this happen this week, maybe even today? Something someone did or said caused you to feel overlooked, insulted, violated, taken advantage of, not considered . . . and you *felt* offended. This feeling is not something you can control. Everyone *feels* offended.

Then, Stage 2 is the *choice* to live or not live offended. This is the stage that many people are unaware of. They assume that feeling offended leaves them with no choice but to live offended. However, just because you feel offended, doesn't mean you have to live offended.

Stage 1 is about someone giving you an opportunity to be offended; they hand you a big glass of offense to drink. Stage 2 provides an opportunity to put the drink down before taking a sip. It is your choice to live offended or not. And here's why you don't want to drink from the glass of offense: "Living offended is like drinking poison and expecting the other person to die." In other words, don't take it in . . . don't drink the poison! When you make the choice not to live offended, you're choosing the path to a healthy soul, peaceful mind, and a blessed life. The Offense Test hopes to prove that even when you have a reason or a right to be offended you will repeatedly choose to not be.

Let's take a minute and consider how you have felt when you get in the airspace with someone who is offended. Do you remember how awkward it felt? Do you remember the way their offense affected your ability to have a conversation with them, especially if the conversation brushed up against the sensitivity they wore like a residue on their soul?

Many people are looking for an offense rather than overlooking it.

The reason I'm asking you this is because it's the same way with you. When you carry the toxin of offense from past experiences, healthy people feel it in you, on you, and they will stay away from you. It is impossible for an offended person to have healthy, enjoyable relationships.

I find it helpful to see offense as a trap that can lure you in, captivate your attention and metastasize your spirit, soul, and body. It has to be treated with the same quick response that you would treat a venomous snake bite. If there's no sense of urgency, the poison spreads through your inner being.

To better understand the spiritual nature of offense, the word offense in the New Testament comes from the Greek word, "skandalon," which refers to the trap that a hunter uses to snare his prey. Such is the nature of offense. It is a trap that our enemy uses as a basis for us to let strife into our lives. Offense will bait us and hypnotize our senses, causing us to be unaware of the lingering consequences, while it makes its way into our thought life, our conversations, our emotions, and eventually into our spirit and soul. After that, it will affect a person's physical health. So we may reason that we have a right to be offended and have cause to be hurt or angry but what we fail to realize is that when we allow ourselves to enter into the mental and spiritual state of being trapped by offense, we suffer serious consequences and personal harm.

Offense Is Certain To Happen

. . . .

Even Jesus referred to the certainty of offense when He said, "It is impossible that no offenses should come . . ." (Luke 17:1, NKJV). It's absolutely unavoidable—the opportunity to be offended will present itself repeatedly in your life. Unfortunately, many people are looking for it rather than overlooking it. Have you noticed, in our current social environment, that people feel justified to be offended at anything that offends them? The message is, *you have a right to be offended* without considering the high cost to your well-being. For example, people can go on social media, and because they feel anonymous, they take their right to be offended to a whole new level. They bash what they don't like and attack people they don't know. Everything seems to be a "hot topic." Gender, age, politics, race, law enforcement, people who make too much money, etc. The list can go on and on. Add to this, the usual people or situations that will offend you within your own relationships: friends, family, co-workers, your boss, or even your pastor, will all offend you, at some point in time. In fact, any time you socialize or have contact with other people, opportunities for offense are inevitable.

Below are some relationship principles to help you avoid the offense trap:

1 ACCURATELY DEFINE YOUR ROLE IN THE RELATIONSHIP.

Roles are necessary to maintain order and avoid chaos in life. However, if roles are unclear, the people involved are more vulnerable to offense. When you look at your relationships, accept the importance and value of everyone's roles, rather than ignoring them. Treat everyone, with whom you are acquainted, with dignity and respect. Be conscious of their role in your life and yours in theirs. If you are experiencing tension or conflict in a relationship, it's possible that someone involved is not considering or respecting the roles in that relationship.

2 ASSUME THE BEST ABOUT OTHERS.

Give people the benefit of the doubt. Believe that they mean well or have good intentions, even when we don't understand their actions. Cynicism is the belief that other people's actions are wrongly motivated. Since we are incapable of knowing people's hearts, it's always good to assume the best rather than risk judging them falsely. This keeps us from the offense trap when we don't understand someone's actions.

3 DON'T MEDDLE.

Don't involve yourself in other people's affairs unless you are invited. It's not the act of helping other people that we are avoiding, rather the act of seeking information and creating conversations in other people's matters that are none of your business in the first place. The Bible is clear in giving us wisdom regarding this. The Apostle Paul writes, " . . . You should mind your own business and work with your hands, just as we told you," (1 Thessalonians 4:11, NIV).

Our sphere of concern is usually larger than our sphere of influence. To avoid offending and being offended, we should concentrate on and stay within our sphere of influence. For example, you may have a friend who confides in you about his or her troubled marriage. They may disclose secrets that their spouse would not want you to hear. Rather than forming an opinion based on one side of the story, encourage your friend to go to a professional counselor or minister and get help. If you're not a counselor, don't try to be one. The best thing a friend can do is continue to be a friend (listen, pray, encourage, offer biblical wisdom) and not meddle. Your sphere of influence is in being a friend. Even as a pastor, I'm slow to get involved with people's lives unless I'm certain that I should. There are always factors to consider, don't just rush in.

4 EXAMINE YOUR EXPECTATIONS OF OTHERS.

Consider the story of John the Baptist. He was Jesus' cousin and prepared the way for His ministry. In the process, he ended up being beaten and imprisoned as Jesus went around preaching, healing, and gaining a following. During this time, John sent two of his disciples to ask Jesus: "Are You the Coming One, or do we look for another?" (Matthew 11:3, NKJV). John said this because he was looking at his circumstance and very possibly allowing resentment and offense to sit in his spirit. Based on the story, we could assume that he was having thoughts like *I was here first. Why is He getting all the attention? Why am I the one that is actually suffering for the cause?* Jesus answered with, "Go and tell John the things which you hear and see: The blind see and the lame walk; the lepers are cleansed and the deaf hear; the dead are raised up and the poor have the gospel preached to them. And blessed is he who is not offended because of Me." (Matthew 11:4–6, NKJV).

For the sake of this illustration, let's assume the inferred message of what Jesus said could be: *"Blessed is he who is not offended because of something I'm doing or not doing that seems unfair or inconsiderate to them."* John seems to be feeling offended from prison. He did so much for Jesus. He proclaimed Him as the One. He fearlessly preached Jesus, the Messiah, to the crowds of people who followed him. John baptized his cousin, and now Jesus is being celebrated while John is left in a dark, dirty prison feeling lonely and forgotten. Have you ever had someone around you blessed in ways that you felt you should be blessed? Did it seem unfair to you? If you answered yes to either of these questions, you may have experienced the *feeling* offense through unfulfilled expectations.

THE NUMBER ONE REASON PEOPLE LIVE OFFENDED IS UNFULFILLED EXPECTATIONS. UNFULFILLED EXPECTATIONS CAN MANIFEST IN THESE THREE AREAS:

1 Unspoken expectations
2 Unmet expectations
3 Unrealistic expectations

Unspoken expectations are things we hope to see happen, but we don't actually express the hope for one reason or another. In some scenarios, if the person said what they were hoping to see happen, it would make them appear selfish, disloyal, or inconsiderate ... so they make sure not to say it even though they have a secret hope in process of becoming an expectation. Think about how many marriages have suffered from both men and women who are unable to verbalize their wants, desires, or expectations openly with one another. Or, consider the person who has been working at a job for four years and hears about a promotion opening up in the office. They get energized and spend the next several months going above and beyond, trying to get the opportunity without telling anyone. Only to find out that someone who has only been working there for a year got the position instead of them.

Unmet expectations happen when something doesn't go like you planned, or when someone isn't who you thought they were. An easy way to explain this is when a child sees a piece of candy right at eye level in the grocery store. In their mind, the candy is already theirs, but when they turn to their parent for the confirmation that it is in fact their candy, they are faced with the reality that the candy will not be going home with them. Whether you're a parent or not, you've seen what can happen to a child when this happens: tears, sobs, sometimes rolling on the ground. But this is what happens within each and every one of us when we don't get what we want and we allow the poison of offense to pour into our minds.

For you, this might have been a birthday that went unnoticed or a friend that decided not to continue to be your friend like you planned. Maybe you're the type of person who creates five year plans, and you're at year four with nothing looking like what you expected. Unmet expectations can lead to resentment, frustration, and we can hold onto offense even toward God for not making it happen.

Unrealistic expectations come from when you presume to know more than you could possibly know and create impossible expectations in your mind for a person or a situation. You can probably think of times when you were so sure that something was right only to find out that you were wrong. We're human. We don't have all the answers, but the minute we begin to think we do is the minute we

It is always best to allow margin for what you don't know.

put ourselves in a vulnerable place where offense comes quickly and easily. You have to leave room for what you do not know. I, personally, can make all the assumptions in the world why someone cut me off today in traffic or why that business I've been going to for years gave me an experience that was not good. I have to remind myself over and over again that I don't know what that person or business is going through and I should not presume to know.

For example, if you've never been a business owner, you don't know what it's like to hire and train employees, create the best customer service, or manage the bottom line. I've never served in the military, served in government, or owned an airline and would never enter a conversation acting as if I knew everything about what those roles involve. But sometimes, we'll see a 10-minute spot on the news or other media outlets about a topic that we know nothing about, and suddenly, we have become the expert and now know who should have done what . . . based on very limited knowledge. It is always best to allow margin for what you don't know.

Unspoken, unmet, and unrealistic expectations are easy for any of us to stumble into without realizing it. When we do, we are an offense waiting to happen. Maybe you've been in a situation where you feel like someone could do something for you to help you and they don't. Thoughts we think sound like, "They could easily do this . . . only if they would." Or, "They could easily write a check and help me, only if they would." Or, "They could refer my business to all of their friends, only if they would." These expectations serve us a big fat glass of offense and gives us every reason to drink it! Learning to live free of offense is a muscle many have never used or exercised, which is why some people have offense on top of offense in their life.

Learning to not be offended and putting your confidence in God may be new territory for you. If we go back to Jesus and John the Baptist we see that they are good friends/relatives working together in purpose and destiny, and they genuinely loved one another, even though they may have had to overcome an offense or two. Jesus knew at one point that John had began to question why Jesus had allowed him to be stuck in prison rather than using His divine power to free him. It seems that in scripture, John had reasoned that Jesus had overlooked him rather than come to his side and rescue him from prison. Jesus sent a message to John saying "blessed is the one who is not offended in me," (Matthew 11:6, ESV). This is true for the body of Christ as well. As we become part of God's family and members of His church, we will work together in purpose and destiny. It's essential as we do this, we will all have opportunities to be offended at others and even at God. This is when it's important that we remember Jesus' words, "blessed is the one who is not offended because of something that myself or someone else is doing or not doing that seems unfair or inconsiderate to them."

The Trap Is Also A Test
. . . .

An opportunity for offense is not only a trap, it is also a test. God observes us during the hard and difficult times of our lives. Like I've said earlier in this book: testing always precedes promotion. The ability to rise above feelings of hurt or resentment and genuinely forgive others is followed by God's promotion in our lives. There is a difference between a temporary feeling of offense and a mental and spiritual state of being offended. The temporary feeling of offense may happen before you realize it, like someone pouring you a glass full of poison. There are times when it will be unavoidable. The state of being offended, however, is what happens when you do not make the choice to free yourself of the offense. The problem with living offended is that it doesn't hurt someone else, it hurts you. They don't suffer loss, you do. They don't live with your envy, anger, jealousy, bitterness, you do.

Signs that you drank the poison of offense and you are moving into a state of being offended are below:

- Incidents consume your thoughts.
- Incidents affect your sleep.
- You find yourself daydreaming about the incident.
- You have growing feelings of anger and resentment about the incident.
- You find yourself doing things that prove you are not getting over the incident (leaving your church, telling someone off, desiring to get even, etc.).

So, what do we do? The enticing glass of offense has been poured, and we feel offended. What we do next after we *feel* offended is crucial to our souls. This is where we get bitter or we get better.

Matthew 18 describes the two sides of an offense. Jesus condemns those who offend or cause others to sin whether it's intentional or not. Then, He cautions us to be careful with what we allow ourselves to do and to think. When I read the text, I hear Jesus saying, "Do whatever you have to do. Go to drastic measures and extreme decisiveness to avoid offenses in your life." It's okay to feel offended. But, we are encouraged not to *live* offended. There are times that offense seems justified. For example, someone physically abused you or someone you know is never ok behavior, and yet you were not created to be offended. It's toxic and leaves us in a state of brokenness until we can deal with the emotions, the anger, and the resentments. It doesn't make what happened okay, but if you pass the glass of offense and choose not to live offended it gives you an opportunity to move forward.

So many people today are living miserable, lonely lives because they have allowed themselves to fall into the trap of offense. You can't change what has happened, but you can change how you are responding to it. You can decide today that you will "pour out" all those wrong feelings you have and free yourself of offense. In the medical world, people go through detox procedures that clear dangerous, life-threatening levels of alcohol, drugs, and poisons.[8] It doesn't help to be bitter. Maybe it's time for you to go through an offense detox to be able to live a healthy life. Finding forgiveness is the ultimate detox, whether it's with yourself, someone else, or with God.

Living Unoffended

. . . .

There's a promise that we can turn to in these moments when we're trying to find the strength. It's in Psalm 119, and the writer is believed to be David, who in his lifetime, had plenty of moments to feel and be offended. But here's what he says, "Great peace have they which love thy law: and nothing shall offend them," (Psalm 119:165, KJV). God gives us peace when we focus on His word and use that to walk through our lives. The people who choose to live without offense will enjoy great peace. However, those who allow offenses to pile up within them will not know peace. These people are troubled in mind and spirit. But the people who live without offense have great and lasting peace in their lives. I had to draw a line in the sand and decide that someone would have to work hard in order to offend me. If you want to offend me, it's going to have to be a deliberate and serious offense. And my plan, even then, is to get over it!

Being unoffendable is living a lifestyle of forgiveness. It's making the same choice over and over again to not hold on to offense. The Bible says, "For you were called to freedom, brothers. Only do not use your freedom as an opportunity for the flesh, but through love serve one another," (Galatians 5:13, ESV). Fight for the freedom you've been given to live unoffended. Make freedom your goal. A healthy diet of prayer, verbally releasing the offense and declaring that, just like Jesus forgave you, you will forgive others. Release prayers of freedom and grace. Christ has made us free. Live in the joy and freedom of the unoffended life.

So, the next time you have a reason to be offended, pass the test by refusing to take the opportunity, because the greater your ability to avoid offense, the more God can use you.

Think-it-Out
. . . .

☐ Describe a time when you handled offense well and another time not so well.

....

☐ What types of expectations do you struggle with the most: unspoken, unmet, or unrealistic?

....

☐ What does living unoffended look like for you specifically?

....

☐ Write down one person's name that you need to forgive.

....

....

....

....

....

....

Live-it-Out
. . . .

☐ Think about a moment where you drank a poison of offense, and assess where you could have reacted differently.

☐ Write a letter to one person you haven't forgiven or think of one moment that you haven't gotten over. Actually sending it is up to you.ct with your family, co-workers or friends at school?

☐ Memorize Proverbs 19:11 and let it help you pass the Offense Test.

"A person's wisdom yields patience; it is to one's glory to overlook an offense."

Proverbs 19:11

8
The Test of Time

THIS TEST COMES TO PROVE YOUR ENDURANCE, PATIENCE, AND ONGOING CONFIDENCE IN VARIOUS SEASONS OF LIFE.

The Question: Do You Get Better Or Bitter With Time?

. . . .

Jesus said to them, "My time has not yet come, but your time is always here."

John 7:6, NIV

Jesus did many good things with His time. He taught His disciples, healed the sick, drove out demons, and fed the hungry. He spent time traveling and He spent time staying in one spot. He spent time with the crowd and spent time in solitude. He spent time celebrating with those He loved and time mourning after losing them. He slowed down and took His time, but He also spoke and acted with driving urgency. Jesus spent the last three years of His life revealing His identity as the Son of God, and spent the first 30 years of His life as a carpenter.

Ultimately, Jesus passed the Test of Time as He accomplished everything the Father had sent Him do in just 33 years here on Earth. The tests of time for you and I will not come to an end until our time is up. But a Test of Time is a good place to be, because it means we still have some left.

It's Your Time, It's Your Turn

One of the most challenging things for Sheila and me to do is to pick a movie to watch. We've been married for 40 years, and on more than one occasion, we've started out finding a movie by looking at different movie previews to help us pick, only to spend so much time looking at previews that we ended up not starting a movie at all!

Some people live their lives as if they are in that previews stage. They convince themselves that real life won't start until they accomplish some milestone in the future like finishing high school or college, or when they get married, or when they own a home, and the list of when life will start could go on and on. This person is failing the test of time, because they are still on the sidelines waiting to be called into the game.

You don't have to live as if you will start your life when _____ happens. You are currently living in the time of your greatest potential—right now! It's your time; it's your turn! And, what you do with your turn affects what happens in your time.

The story of Esther in the Bible is a great example of someone who did what she could with what she had, when she had it. Early in her life, Esther became an orphan, and she was raised by her older cousin, Mordecai. If being an orphan wasn't enough heartache, Esther was also a young Jewish woman living in exile in Persia. As a young woman, her poise and beauty caught the attention of those on

We can't
do anything
about the
past, but
**we can do
something**
about the
future.

assignment to find a new queen for the big-time King of the Persian empire, who ruled over 127 provinces. For one year, Esther went through a preparation stage, and then it was her turn to meet the king, which happens in chapter two of the book of Esther. Through the selection process she became the new queen.

Shortly after that, a corrupt leader on the king's cabinet named Haman decided it was time to kill off the Jewish people who lived in the provinces of Persia. Through manipulation and deception, he started the process of an all-out genocide.

That's when Mordecai said these famous words to Esther: "For if you remain silent at this time, relief and deliverance for the Jews will arise from another place, but you and your father's family will perish. And who knows but that you have come to your royal position for such a time as this?" (Esther 4:14, NIV).

Just like Esther embraced her time, we are currently living in the time of our greatest potential. Your time is not over, and you are not waiting for your time to come. We are currently living in our time. You and I can't do anything about the past, but we can do something about the future. We can't do much about our ancestors, but we can have a huge effect on our children. There's not much we can do about our history, but there's a lot we can do to influence our legacy.

The Unfolding Of Your Potential

On Valentine's Day every year, florists around the nation are searching for roses that are at the "unfolding" stage. These flowers must be given time to open. You cannot speed up the process by grabbing the rose pedals and pulling it open. To do so is to risk permanent damage to an otherwise "perfect in its own time" rose. The proper use of time is essential if the rose is going to reach its full potential.

Not only can the process not be rushed, but the rose needs specific forms of nurturing while in the process. The atmosphere, the soil, and the water are all preparing the rose and contributing to the maturity and unfolding process. While the someday, fully developed rose may be what people see and admire most; it is the nourishment, preparation, and time that determine the unfolding of that potential. People are much the same way. In order to achieve our full potential, not only do we need to prepare right now, but we also need the proper amount of time to mature.

Don't live in the "someday" of your potential. Take your turn right now and live in your today potential. You see the question is not just what will you do someday . . . the question is what are you doing right now to prepare yourself for your destiny? We need to be less worried about what will be our turn to do tomorrow, focus on what is our turn to do today, and let time and preparation unfold our fullest potential. Whether you feel like you are at the beginning of the "unfolding" stage, or you are feeling close to reaching the full measure of your potential, you can trust that "God has made everything beautiful for its own time," (Ecclesiastes 3:11, NLT). If you stay obedient to this process and embrace the idea of preparing yourself now, then at one time or another, and in one way or another, that rose of potential will unfold in your life.

A Window Of Time

Life is God's gift to me—what I do with it is my gift to God. In the book of Ephesians, the Apostle Paul wrote to the church to "make the most of every opportunity," (Ephesians 5:16, NLT). The truth is, every opportunity has a window of time in which to take advantage of it.

Most people get so distracted with the urgent matters of daily living that they miss the more important opportunities of a lifetime. The urgent matters press in on us—things like crossing off every item on today's list, making it on time to every event on our overbooked schedules, and making sure we checked every email in our inbox.

The important matters of life such as building a strong family, our spiritual development, our physical health, or financial planning seem to emerge less often. It may come to our attention when we hear of close friends who are getting divorced, attend a funeral, or experience a financial crisis. It's in those moments of life that we are provided a window of time that we may purpose to give more attention to our own relationship with God, our family, or commit to a financial growth plan for our future.

The truth is that the windows of time for life's best opportunities present themselves more often than we think. Here are some windows you could be in right now:

THE WINDOW TO:

obtain an education

be a young man
or woman of God

honor your parents

choose a career

experience what it is
like to be single

find your spouse

love your spouse and
build a happy rela-
tionship with them

increase wealth

plan for retirement
successfully

handle transitions

teach your children

prevent health problems
in your future

learn from a
recent failure

know
certain people better

love your grandchildren

thank certain people

leave a legacy

Passing the Test of Time means that we seize the opportunities of a lifetime while we have the open window.

It's Okay To Want

. . . .

Delight yourself in the Lord, and He will give you the desires of your heart.

Psalm 37:4, ESV

One of the reasons some Christians don't make the proper use of time is that they are indifferent to their own desires. They spend a lifetime suppressing the desires of their heart, rather than allowing those desires to inspire them to greatness. There are desires born of our flesh that will hinder us from a life of worth and value. There are also desires in our heart that are given by God to guide us into our destiny.

When a person suppresses all their desires, they lose their way in life. When David said, "the Lord is my shepherd, I shall not want" (Psalm 23:1, KJV) some people may think he was renouncing his own desires. In reality, however, he was proclaiming God's promise of provision in his life—that his want would be satisfied. Some of life's best opportunities, listed above, may be in the top ten want list for your life. Giving yourself the green light to be inspired by your wants can help you make the proper use of your time.

After giving yourself the green light to have desires, the next step is to prioritize your wants. This will take you beyond an admission of many wants and will force you to declare what you want the most. It's easy for all of us to be taken off course from the things that are most important to us. If a boat leaves Seattle headed for Hong Kong, the captain must continually adjust its course based on wind, waves, and other conditions. To be only slightly off course while enroute can become hundreds of miles off course over the length of the journey. The captain must continually monitor the ship's course and not allow the ship to drift out of line with his desired destination.

The same is true in our lives. We must be focused on the things that we want most. Slight variations of our energy and time today can make a big difference on where we arrive ten years from now. Knowing your priorities and keeping them in daily focus will help to keep you on target with your desired destination.

Vision Is Vital

Passing the Test of Time will require you to have vision for where you want to go. In the example above, the captain had to know where the destination was in order to know how and when to course correct. Having and communicating vision with those around you is also important. My daughter, Jodi, and I were recently trying to meet up at the same place. When she said, "I'll meet you there," it turns out that her "there" was different than my "there," and we ended up in two different places. The truth is that we are all going "there." But some of us have not clearly defined where "there" is or have not communicated it to those around us.

When we lock in on a vision for our future, something happens to the way we see our present and how we spend our time. Whether it's for your individual life or your church or community, having a vision is the catalyst for your future.

Jesus repeatedly affirmed that He knew where He was going, what His destiny was, and why He was doing it. His vision and destiny fueled His daily decisions and how He spent His time. It even caused Him to be in the right places at the right times. Ultimately, the clarity of vision allowed Jesus to do all the Father had sent Him to accomplish. You may think that you are lacking the skills, discipline, or time currently to achieve greatness. But it could be that you are lacking the vision to direct your skill development or the vision to motivate your discipline, or vision to dictate how you manage your time.

The Power Of A Plan

"For I know the plans I have for you," declares the Lord, "plans to prosper you and not to harm you, plans to give you hope and a future."

Jeremiah 29:11, NIV

God makes plans. The moment that sin entered the world, God made a plan for you and I to be restored to His original intention and receive salvation. The moment God chose Abraham and His descendants to be His chosen people He had a plan on how it was going to happen and when it was going to happen. When the Israelites were in exile after they failed to follow God's ways of doing things, He made a plan for them to make their way back. God has a plan for you. Now you just need to plan in agreement with God's plans to see them fulfilled in your life. Once you have a God-given vision inside of your heart, it is time to make a plan. Be careful to avoid the following planning mistakes:

MISTAKE #1

To have no plan

This is a "whatever will be will be" mentality rather than a "whatever will be is influenced by me" mindset. How can you hit a target that does not exist? It's common for people to not have a plan to reach their desired destiny, which may be the reason so few do. The Bible encourages us to make plans, "But he who is noble plans noble things, and on noble things, he stands," (Isaiah 32:8, ESV).

MISTAKE #2

To not include others while planning

Most people are willing to include others in their planning, but don't know how. One time, two homeless men were sitting on a park bench discussing their bad situation when one said, "I'm sitting here, because I listened to nobody." The other one replied, "I'm here, because I listened to everybody." When you include others in your planning process, it's important to use their counsel wisely and with discretion. Wisdom is usually found in the collection of various thoughts consolidated together rather than in one individual's advice. Your unique situation is not a carbon copy of anyone's previous situation. Realize that, collectively, your advisers help you plan wisely. In Proverbs, it says, "Plans fail for lack of counsel, but with many advisers, they succeed," (Proverbs 15:22, NIV).

MISTAKE #3

To not include God when planning

Again, I don't think it's a matter of not *wanting* to—but a matter of not knowing *how* to include God that hinders most people. This mistake is addressed in the writings of James, "Now listen you who say, 'Today or tomorrow we will go to this or that city, spend a year there, carry on business and make money.' Why, you do not even know what will happen tomorrow. What is your life? You are a mist that appears for a little while and then vanishes. Instead, you ought to say, 'If it is the Lord's will, we will live and do this or that,'" (James 4:13–15, NIV).

The teaching here is not against a plan for tomorrow, but rather, an emphasis to plan and include God in the plan. Notice again that verse 15 tells us to proclaim our plans for tomorrow while leaving room and staying flexible for God's will to be accomplished.

Seeking what you want through planning is another important key in the proper use of time. Most of us have had to sit in meetings that did not have a planned agenda. Inevitably, little if anything was accomplished. We've all experienced a difference in learning when a teacher plans for the class versus flying by the seat of their pants. In those situations, nobody likes to feel they are wasting their time. The big picture of life must be planned also if time is valuable enough not to waste it.

Think Long-Term

People who pass the Test of Time learn to think both in short and long-term. These people greatly consider how their thoughts, words, actions, behaviors, and choices today will affect them down the road. A long-term thinker, for example, will make positive health choices now, so they have a better chance at being healthy later. At a young age, a long-term thinker will make decisions like nobody else by being disciplined in their finances so that they can benefit like nobody else later as they enjoy having great wealth.

Long-term thinkers are also able to trust God during times of waiting, preparation, and sometimes even hardship, knowing there is a purpose behind these seasons where our patience is tested. Usually we cannot see what exactly that purpose is while we are being tested, but if you ever have experienced seasons like this, you know what I am talking about. If not, consider these biblical examples:

- Noah prepared the ark for over 50 years before the predicted rains fell.
- Abraham and Sarah waited 25 years for their promised son.
- Joseph waited 14 years in prison for a crime he did not commit.
- David waited 15 years between the time he was anointed to become King over Israel and when he was finally recognized by the nation as King.
- The Jewish men and women were in exile for 70 years as their hearts and minds were prepared to make a return to Jerusalem and a nationwide revival.
- Paul prepared for 15 years between his calling and his first missionary journey, and another 5 until he writes his first New Testament letter.

Think about all that God did within these men and women during their period of waiting and preparation. Would they have been able to handle God's calling and God's blessings had they not gone through that season of waiting? Their faith, trust, obedience, and skills were all being developed as God sculpted them into who they needed to be in order to accomplish what God had set them apart to do. What is God wanting to do within you as you wait and prepare for His promises to be fulfilled in your life?

Aging With Time

. . . .

Time affects people differently. Some people are like milk, they get bitter with time. Others are like wine, they get better with time. The milk people have a short life span of:

Interest—they are easily distracted.
Motivation—they run out of inspiration quickly.
Confidence—their attention gets turned
toward the negative.
Determination—they start well but never finish.

Great ideas will always turn sour in the mind of a milk person. Great opportunities repeatedly curdle for a milk person. These people have not allowed time to work to their advantage. As soon as something is familiar, they begin to lose appreciation for it. Whether it's a job or a new relationship, milk people do well as long as something is new to them. Over time, however, things for them have a tendency to spoil. This loss of interest and appreciation soon leads to inconsistencies and their enthusiasm dwindles until, of course, something new comes along. Then the process is repeated.

If you want to age better with time, it will take some effort to shift your perspective. Periodically, it's important to get a new improved perspective in one or more areas of our lives.

Perspective of our self
Perspective of our spouse
Perspective of our church
Perspective of our job

Since there's always more than one way to look at everything, chances are that even as you read this line, you are in need of a better, more God-like perspective in one or more areas of your life. An important key to happiness over time is not only getting what you want, but also wanting what you get. To be continually aware that:

I *want* my family.
I *want* this day.
I *want* my career.
I *want* my church.
I *want* my marriage.
I *want* this challenge.

This ability to want what you have can be lost by looking through the lens of bad experiences, frustration, or personal weariness. The new perspective of genuine appreciation for what you have is the perspective of those who are champions in life. These people pass the Test of Time by not allowing their blessings to become so common that they fail to recognize and appreciate them.

Dealing With Disappointment

Greg Norman, otherwise known as "The Great White Shark[9]," was one of pro golf's most talented and celebrated players. He spent 331 weeks as the number one ranked golfer in the world during the 1980s and 90s. In 1995, Norman was the top money winner, but going into 1996, he had never won a major tournament on American soil. He repeatedly (seven times) had placed second in these major events and had developed a reputation for not winning the big ones. In the 1996 Masters, it appeared he would change that by finally winning the prestigious title. He shot some of the best golf ever played in the history of the Masters for the first three days of the tournament. However, on the last and final day, disaster hit his game, and he recorded what is perhaps the biggest disappointment in golf history. Sports programs, newspapers, and magazines made it the headline story for several days, saying things like "Norman folds, Norman chokes" etc . . .

Because he was so popular in the golfing world, people everywhere were feeling sorry for him. It would have been understandable if he had felt sorry for himself. Everyone would have accepted Norman as only being normal if he had refused to speak to media, expressed self-doubt, or neglected to compliment others who had played well that day. But Norman is not normal. He's a class "A" champion golfer. On the day of the big disappointment, he showed the courage and optimism that had led him to so much

Never allow a disappointment to steal the joys of life.

success. In his post-game interviews, he spoke with ease and confidence. He was gracious, kind and saw beyond the present disappointment. In fact, his words were inspiring. He said, " . . . I'm a winner. I lost today, but I'm not a loser in life. I've won golf tournaments. There's people who would want to win as many as I have . . . maybe the things I have done to myself are for a reason. Maybe something really good is waiting to happen to me down the road. This is just a test,[10] " (Greg Norman on APRIL 14, 1996).

How we handle disappointment is crucial in the Test of Time. It makes some bitter and some better. Never allow a disappointment to steal the joys of life. As hard as the disappointment may feel today, it may very well be the test you must pass to a greater tomorrow. In the end, the sum of our lives is not a result of what happens to us, but rather, how we deal with it. Deal well with disappointment, and time will be on your side.

It's Not Too Late

Sometimes we can look at the Test of Time and project shame and guilt on ourselves because of the mistakes we have made with our time up until this point. If you still have time left, if you are still breathing, it is not too late. Jesus did not start His ministry until age 30, and in just three years, He changed the world forever. Zechariah and Elizabeth brought John the Baptist into the world despite the fact that they "were both very old," (Luke 1:7, NIV).

Maybe you think it's too late to answer God's call on your life because you have ignored it for so long that surely God has given up on using you.

The good news is God's grace and long-suffering lasts longer than your entire lifetime. He waited 120 years before bringing the floodwaters on the Earth after He saw that "every inclination of the thoughts of the human heart was only evil all the time," (Genesis 6:5, NIV). He waited over 400 years before allowing Abraham's descendants to go take the land of Canaan because the current inhabitants' sin had "not yet reached its full measure," (Genesis 15:16, NIV).

The Psalmist said, "But You, O Lord, are a God merciful and gracious, Slow to anger and abundant in lovingkindness and truth," (Psalm 86:15, NASB). God described Himself to Moses as, " . . . merciful and gracious, longsuffering, and abounding in goodness and truth, keeping mercy for thousands, forgiving iniquity and transgression and sin," (Exodus 34:6–7, NIV). God continued to use David after he committed adultery, Peter after he abandoned Jesus, and Paul after he murdered and persecuted Christians. I may not know what your past looks like, but I can tell you that if you are facing the Test of Time it is because you still have some left, so make the most of it.

Think-it-Out

· · · · · · · · · · · · · ·

☐ Is it easier for you to think short term or long term? Why?

....

☐ How are you preparing now for a time in the future? What are you doing right now to prepare yourself for your destiny?

....

☐ Do you get frustrated when things do not happen in the time you would like? Would you consider yourself as someone who compares yourself to where others are at? How does that affect your attitude toward your calling?

....

☐ Write down some things you can do to help gain a better perspective. (Including: perspectives of our self, our spouse, our church, our job or school, etc.)

....

....

....

....

Live-it-Out

. . . .

☐ What is something you can do this week to start living with a better perspective for yourself, your spouse, church, job, school, and others?

....

☐ Make a list of God's character traits. How do those character traits help you in the Test of Time.

....

☐ Memorize James 4:13–15 to help you pass the Test of Time.

Now listen, you who say, "Today or tomorrow we will go to this or that city, spend a year there, carry on business and make money." Why, you do not even know what will happen tomorrow. What is your life? You are a mist that appears for a little while and then vanishes. Instead, you ought to say, "If it is the Lord's will, we will live and do this or that."

James 4:13-15

9
The Lordship
Test

THIS TEST OCCURS WHEN YOU ARE IN A POSITION OR SITUATION WHERE YOU MUST CHOOSE TO OBEY GOD OVER YOUR PERSONAL PREFERENCE AND NATURAL INSTINCTS.

The Question: Do You Accept That God's Way Is Always Right?

··

Not My will, but Yours be done.

Luke 22:42, NIV

J ust after the Last Supper and the first communion, Jesus faced a crossroad. With the pain and suffering of the cross just hours away, He had a choice to make: deny His flesh and submit to the Father's will, or submit to His flesh and deny the Father's will. In a moment of confession, He tells three of His disciples, "My soul is overwhelmed with sorrow to the point of death," (Matthew 26:38, NIV). After telling them to keep watch, He went into the garden and "He fell with His face to the ground and prayed, 'My Father, if it is possible, may this cup be taken from me. Yet not as I will, but as you will,'" (Matthew 26:39, NIV). Jesus' natural human instincts were telling Him to run away from what the Father had asked Him to do on the cross.

This is the tension of the Lordship Test. Some of what God tells you to do is going to contradict your own instincts, and if you give into your flesh and ignore the authority and instruction of God, you will never experience all the blessings that God has for you, and you will not complete all that God has created you to accomplish.

Thankfully for us, Jesus passed the Lordship Test, and His life's work has become an example for all of us. This is the test that proves how much you let God be the Leader and the Lord of your everyday life. At what point, or in which situation, do you waver in your confidence to approach your life exactly like you know God would want you to?

Trust In God

Every four years, we find ourselves back in the voting booths ready to elect or re-elect another president, and for believers, it is yet another opportunity to pass or fail the Lordship Test. Because without fail, you will hear believers from every political party begin to panic as if God is up for election, or as if God is about to lose the majority in the Senate. The same panic ensues when our world faces major turmoil, controversies, and tragedies. We should always be a people that strive to take action and influence progress in our communities, but we should always remember that God does not belong to a political party, and He is not panicking over the story on the evening news, or the trending topic on social media. Are we worried that God does not have experience with seeing His people through difficult times? Trust me when I say God has not ran out of capacity to work all things out for the good of those who are called according to His purpose (Romans 8:28, NIV). We are talking about the same God that delivered His people from slavery at the hands of the Egyptians, saw them through the battles to take the Promised Land against overwhelming odds, brought them back to their homes after multiple stents in exile, brought Jesus into the world in the middle of Roman occupation, and has now grown His great church to billions when only 2000 years ago all His original 12 followers faced persecution to the point of death. Our trust in God is not based off of current events. When we do not trust in God after experiencing results we do not agree with, it can turn into disobedience as we try to manipulate the results. It can also lead to us participating in the negative conversations that surround us. Let's turn any anxieties we have over what is going on in our society, in our communities, and on the political scene, into acts of trust in God.

The Battle Of The Believer

If we are not careful, we can let God's sovereignty and knowledge of His Lordship turn into passivity on our part as we fail to take action thinking that God will just take care of it. For centuries, theologians have debated about the tension between God's sovereignty and the free will of man, as well as which of these forces determine our future. This is what I like to call a "dumb dichotomy." It is not one or the other, it is both. God's will is that we would will His will. So while we take comfort that God is in control, we must take great honor and pride in the fact that we have an opportunity to carry out His plans and purposes here on

God's will
is that we
would will
His will.

Earth. So how, as believers, should we battle and fight for the things we believe in? How should we influence positive change in our communities or stand up for what is right? The Israelites faced this same tension as they moved forward into the Promised Land and found themselves waging war differently than their enemies. In some of his final instructions, Moses encouraged his people, "When you go to war against your enemies and see horses and chariots and an army greater than yours, do not be afraid of them, because the Lord your God, who brought you up out of Egypt, will be with you," (Deuteronomy 20:1, NIV). The context here is that the armies that the Israelites faced were armed with four-horse chariots—a very intimidating weapon and tactical advantage, and the Israelites did not have the same weapon. It would be similar to a modern-day infantry with no artillery going up against a division that was armed with tanks. But Moses was reminding them that the Egyptians, whom they had previously defeated and escaped from, also had chariots. And the same God that delivered them from the hands of the Egyptians is the same God that was going to be with them in the battles that were ahead.

For us today, the same is true. The same God that was with the Israelites then is with us now. The same God that defeated death in the resurrection of Jesus is with us today. So in the middle of what may seem like doom and destruction, we remember that we do not need to fight battles the same way the world wages war. The social media temper tantrums, the negative conversations and dishonoring language, the lies and deception, the abuse of those around us to achieve our own goals, these are all ways that the world may try to claim victory, but this is not our way. Moses went on to tell his people, " . . . Do not be faint-hearted or afraid; do not panic or be terrified. For the Lord your God is the one who goes with you to fight for you against your enemies to give you victory," (Deuteronomy 20:3–4, NIV). As the Psalmist said, "Some trust in chariots and some in horses, but we trust in the name of the Lord our God," (Psalm 20:7, NIV). Passing the Lordship Test will require us to trust in the ways of God as we love and pray for our enemies instead of tearing them down on social media. It requires that we stay true to who we are and avoid negativity as we seek to spread light into the darkness. We do not need the weapons of this world, and we do not need to target individuals as if they are the source of darkness. As the Apostle Paul said, "we are not fighting against flesh-and-blood enemies, but against evil rulers and authorities of the unseen world, against mighty powers in this dark world, and against evil spirits in the heavenly places," (Ephesians 6:12, NLT). We can be part of the solution, but passing the Lordship Test requires that we fight our battles God's way.

God Is Always Right

When I invited one of our neighbors to church years ago, he stated his plans for his daughter's future. He said that he intended to send her to a variety of religious services while she was young so that she could develop an openness towards all beliefs. As he shared his philosophy with me, my mind flashed to my teenage days when my own mother warned me that, "If I became too open-minded, there was a danger that my brain would fall out." Although this neighbor thinks he is doing his daughter a great favor and I understand his intentions, I could not help but feel how unfortunate it was that she would not receive clear and definite spiritual guidance from her father. Let's be reasonable:

- What if he approached her education the same way?
- What if he let her choose her behavior and provided no guidance?
- Why not let her decide which foods to eat after taking a sample taste of all of them?

If he did this, could he expect more than an un-educated, misbehaving, unhealthy child? Unfortunately, unless there is a change, this daughter will have a weak, undeveloped faith in God. Her future will have "absolutes" in other areas but be void of understanding and direction in the ways of God. A verification of His Lordship in our lives is our belief that God is always right. It's inconceivable to us to think of buying a new automobile and ignore the instructions of the owner's manual. To disregard these important guidelines for operation and maintenance would threaten our safety and jeopardize the condition of the vehicle. In fact, most warranties are valid based on the owner's observation and adherence to the manual. Well, the Bible is the owner's manual of life. A dedicated observation and adherence to its instructions will bring maximum results. In Joshua 1:8, we are given some guarantees when it comes to God's word: "Do not let this Book of the Law depart from your mouth, meditate on it day and night, so that you may be careful to do everything written in it. Then you will be prosperous and successful," (Joshua 1:8, NIV). When people trust that God is always right and do things His way, they will be successful. On the other hand, disregard or pay no attention to God's guidelines, they lose the benefit of God's guarantee on life.

The "Leaning In" Lifestyle

> *Trust in the Lord with all your heart and lean not on your own understanding; in all your ways submit to Him, and He will make your paths straight.*

Proverbs 3:5-6, NIV

In our ministry, people often approach us with personal stories of powerful transformations after deciding to do things God's way. But when I listen to these stories, they all have something in common: every person first walks into church with a certain "lean." Some people lean into their worries, which prevents them from leaning toward faith in God's promises and faithfulness. Some people lean into their fears, which is only made worse by the spread of bad news through various media outlets. Some people lean into their offense, which prevents them from leaning into church community and godly relationships. Some people lean into their own opinion as they become forceful and defensive anytime their opinion is not the prevailing one. Some people lean into their preferences, which causes them to avoid good things for their life because they do not fit into their preferences. In order to pass the Lordship Test we must make a decision to abandon our tendency to lean on our own understanding and to live a lifestyle of leaning into God's understanding and His way of doing things. The great news is that when we do this, it will allow the following blessings of God to be realized in our lives. The Bible says:

If you fully obey the Lord your God and carefully follow all His commands I give you today, The Lord your God will set you high above all the nations on the earth. All these blessings will come upon you and accompany you if you obey the Lord your God.

Deuteronomy 28:1-2, NIV

1 The Blessing on your Journeys

"You will be blessed in the city and blessed in the country," (Deuteronomy 28:4, NIV).

2 The Blessing on your Descendants

"The fruit of your womb will be blessed . . ." (Deuteronomy 28:4, NIV).

3 The Blessing on your Possessions

". . . and the crops of your land and the young of your livestock—the calves of your herds and the lambs of your flocks. Your basket and your kneading trough will be blessed," (Deuteronomy 28:4–5, NIV).

4 The Blessing on your Battles

"The Lord will grant that the enemies who rise up against you will be defeated before you. They will come at you from one direction but flee from you in seven," (Deuteronomy 28:7, NIV).

5 The Blessing on your Finances

"The Lord will send a blessing on your barns and on everything you put your hand to. The Lord your God will bless you in the land he is giving you . . . The Lord will grant you abundant prosperity—In the fruit of your womb, the young of your livestock and the crops of your ground—in the land He swore to your forefathers to give you. The Lord will open the heavens, the storehouses of His bounty, to send rain on your land in season and to bless all the work of your hands. You will lend to many nations but will borrow from none," (Deuteronomy 28:8, 11–12, NIV).

A Blessing Release—Not A
Blessing Bribe
. . . .

Some people's concept of God's promise to bless obedience is shallow and contrary to God's nature. Here's a typical example of what goes on in some people's minds when they hear that God will bless them if they obey: "Is this God's way to get me to do what He wants—offer me a blessing through a bribe? If God loves me, why doesn't He bless me regardless of what I do?" This thought fails to understand that God does not withhold blessing from anyone. God did, however, create the physical and spiritual universe to respond favorably to corresponding actions. The Bible is simply the instruction manual that informs us of what kind of behavior is "blessed" and what kind of behavior is "cursed." For example, I can tell my 8-year-old grandson to eat right before a game, and he'll feel better, be stronger and faster on the basketball court. Or, I can warn him of how bad he will feel if he eats chocolate bars all day. When I do this, I'm teaching him to comply with his body so that he gets what he wants later. I'm not bribing him to get what I want. I'm instructing him, so he can get what he wants. The outcome is predictable based on how he decides to eat. Likewise, our obedience to the Bible is our obedience to God's knowledge regarding the laws of the universe. We all

God created the physical and spiritual universe to respond favorably to corresponding actions.

have the opportunity to see blessings released in our life as a result of a corresponding action.

Think about how we can walk up to an ATM machine thousands of miles from home, push a code of numbers and get cash to drop from the machine. The machine is not prejudiced to our race, age, lifestyle, or appearance. If you push the right numbers, the machine will release a blessing! Without the right numbers, though, you can stand there all day and scream, holler, complain, or get mad, but you won't get cash. In much the same way, God created the universe to respond with blessings upon the individual whose actions command the release of them. God has established this without any prejudice. He has given everyone the opportunity to live a life of blessing.

Feast Or Famine
. . . .

Many of us are able to recognize the Lordship of God during the times of blessing when we're enjoying the feast. But it is important to remember that God is still Lord during the difficult times in life, when you're feeling the famine. In fact, many of God's blessings are not going to be for the here and now, but for the future and generations to come. In Genesis, we read about this generational blessing in the life of Isaac:

Now there was a famine in the land—besides

the previous famine in Abraham's time—and Isaac went to Abimelek king of the Philistines in Gerar. The Lord appeared to Isaac and said, "Do not go down to Egypt; live in the land where I tell you to live. Stay in this land for a while, and I will be with you and will bless you. For to you and your descendants, I will give all these lands and will confirm the oath I swore to your father Abraham. I will make your descendants as numerous as the stars in the sky and will give them all these lands, and through your offspring all nations on earth will be blessed."

Genesis 26:1-4, NIV

This promise to Isaac required two things. First, Isaac needed to obey God and stay in the land even though there was a famine. He needed to trust that God was also the Lord of the famine. But secondly, God tells Isaac the other reason for this blessing to come when He said that it was "because Abraham obeyed Me and did everything I required of him, keeping My commands, My decrees, and my instructions," (Genesis 26:5, NIV). God is saying to Isaac, "if you don't trust me and leave this area I have instructed you to stay in, then you will put yourself out of position for My blessing that your Father put you in position for." He is essentially saying to Isaac, "I know it is not looking good right now but stay the course and trust me through the famine. Then someday, you will see my blessing unleashed on your family." We go on to read the result in the very same year after Isaac stayed in the land: "Isaac planted crops in that land and the same year reaped a hundredfold, because the Lord blessed him. The man became rich, and his wealth continued to grow until he became very wealthy," (Genesis 26:12–13, NIV).

God used a famine to test Isaac's trust and obedience. But remember, it was also a famine that allowed Joseph to be reunited with his brothers that eventually led to the development of the nation of Israel. It was during a time of famine in the wilderness that God's people had to trust that God would provide food for them each day in the form of manna. Even think about the people who experienced a miracle after they followed Jesus' instruction to sit down as He broke five loaves and two fish into pieces and fed all 15,000 of those who were there.

God can use any and every situation for good whether during the feast or the famine. Jesus said, "My food is to do the will of Him who sent Me and to finish His work. Don't you have a saying, 'It's still four months until harvest?' I tell you, open your eyes and look at the fields! They are ripe for harvest," (John 4:34–36, NIV). If you are in the middle

God can
use any
and every
situation
for good.

of difficult times and you feel like you are in the famine, I want to encourage you to open up your eyes and see what God is doing!

God's Love Language

In his book, *The Five Love Languages*, Gary Chapman explains that there are 5 different categories we all fit into when it comes to feeling love from others. Some of us feel most loved when we receive a gift from someone. Other people feel most loved when they receive words or affirmation, while still others prefer the physical touch of a hug or a kiss from a spouse. I know that sometimes I think I am doing something really nice for my wife, Sheila, and then I wonder why she did not even seem to take much notice to what I did. That is because I was trying to show her love using a language that she does not speak. So what is God's love language? Who better to find the answer from than Jesus. He said in John 14, "Whoever has My commands and keeps them is the one who loves Me. The one who loves Me will be loved by My Father, and I too will love them and show Myself to them," (John 14:31–35, NIV). He said again in John 15, "As the Father has loved Me, so have I loved you. Now remain in My love. If you keep My commands, you will remain in My love, just as I have kept My Father's commands and remain in His love," (John 15:9–11, NIV). I believe that God's love language is obedience. This is how we can show our love to Him, by passing the Lordship Test in our daily lives. I often hear people say, "God knows I love Him." Or "God knows I trust Him." But the truth is love is not known until it is shown, and trust is not known until it is shown. You can pass the Lordship Test by trusting and obeying God no matter the circumstances, and it will not only result in the blessing of God being unleashed in your life, but will also show God our love for Him.

Just For You

. . . .

We started this chapter reading about Jesus' final day before the cross and the tension of the Lordship Test that He faced. With the pain and suffering of the cross just hours away, He had a choice to make: deny His flesh and submit to the Father's will or submit to His flesh and deny the Father's will. As He entered into the Garden of Gethsemane, here are His words to the three disciples that accompanied Him: "My soul is overwhelmed with sorrow to the point of death. Stay here and keep watch with me," (Matthew 26:38, NIV). After He asked His disciples to keep watch and protect Him, He entered the Garden and fell to His face praying, "My Father, if it is possible, may this cup be taken from me. Yet not as I will, but as you will," (Matthew 26:39, NIV). When He returned to where His disciples were supposed to be keeping watch, He found them sleeping! So, He renewed His request of them saying, "Watch and pray so that you will not fall into temptation.

The spirit is willing, but the flesh is weak," (Matthew 26:41, NIV). He then left and prayed again, but this time the prayer was slightly different. "My Father, if it is not possible for this cup to be taken away unless I drink it, may your will be done," (Matthew 26:42, NIV).

You see, when Jesus returned the first time to find His disciples sleeping, He once again came to realize that the cup that needed to be taken away is inside each and every one of us. This force of sin and temptation fights against us as we face the Lordship Test. The forces of sin and darkness do not want you to pass the Lordship Test and submit to God's will, but when Jesus addressed His disciples, He acknowledged that we have this battle within us, "The spirit is willing but the flesh is weak." So when He went back to pray the second time, it changed from "if it is possible, may this cup be taken from me," to "if it is not possible for this cup to be taken away unless I drink it, may your will be done."

Jesus resolved to pass the Lordship Test and become a sacrifice for us not because He knew you would always obey and pass the test, but because He knew you would not! He did it just for you! He did not want to face the suffering on the cross as He paid the penalty of death in our place. He did not want to bear the weight of the sin of the world on His shoulders, but He submitted to the Father's will, which ultimately became Jesus' will. Just as Jesus once told His disciples, "For I have come down from' heaven not to do My will but to do the will of Him who sent Me. And this is the will of Him who sent Me, that I shall lose none of all those He has given Me, but raise them up at the last day," (John 6:38–39, NIV).

If you have found yourself failing the Lordship Test from time to time, understand that when Jesus finds us falling short, it only increases His resolve to raise you up to a place of greater strength and obedience. If you still find yourself in the Lordship Test, know that Jesus is still on your side rooting for you to pass your next exam.

Think-it-Out
. . . .

☐ In what ways do you handle the tension between trusting in God and taking full control?

....

☐ How do you intentionally focus on God in each of these seasons: feast or famine? Give at least 2 examples of each.

....

☐ Does it encourage you that Jesus passed the Lordship Test so that you could to? Name some ways that He accomplished this and how you can apply it to your life.

....

☐ What does it mean to you that Jesus is on your side?

....

☐ Write down a time when you remember disobeying God. And, write down a time when you remember obeying God.

....

....

....

Live-it-Out
. . . .

☐ What are decisions you can make today that will help you obey God faster in the future?

....

☐ Choose one way that you can step toward God's plan this week. This could be getting in God's word more, setting aside prayer time, or joining a Life Group.

....

☐ Memorize Deuteronomy 20:3-4 and proclaim it over your life.

"...Do not be faint-hearted or afraid; do not panic or be terrified. For the Lord your God is the one who goes with you to fight for you against your enemies to give you victory,"

Deuteronomy 20:3-4, NIV

Endnotes

1   Paragraph begins on page 34.

http://www.travelweekly.com/Robert-Silk/
How-1500-hour-rule-created-pilot-shortage

2   Paragraph begins on page 43.

https://archive.org/stream/abrahamlincolnqulinc_33/
abrahamlincolnqulinc_33_djvu.txt

3   Paragraph begins on page 99.

. . . that they may see your good deeds and praise your
Father in heaven. MATTHEW 5:16

4   Paragraph begins on page 110.

https://www.projectmanagement.com/blog-post/3693/
The-Invisible-Lid

5   Paragraph begins on page 154.

https://winstonchurchill.org/resources/
speeches/1940-the-finest-hour/
we-shall-fight-on-the-beaches/

6   Paragraph begins on page 156.

http://www.nba.com/2015/news/features/
fran_blinebury/04/16/houston-rockets-1995-team-can-
any-team-replicate-their-run-from-no-6-seed/

7   Paragraph begins on page 169.

https://www.goodreads.com/quotes/219882-every-ad-versity-every-failure-every-heartache-carries-with-it-the

8   Paragraph begins on page 191.

https://www.health.harvard.edu/staying-healthy/the-dubious-practice-of-detox

9   Paragraph begins on page 214.

http://www.shark.com/the-shark/biography/

10 Paragraph begins on page 214.

Combines quotes from these two articles:

The Guardian: https://www.theguardian.com/sport/1996/apr/16/golf.daviddavies

The Washington Post: https://www.washingtonpost.com/archive/politics/1996/04/15/golfs-master-of-heart-break/0ae3cb9b-a2b4-4f0d-bc1b-12f0ce07c9a0/?utm_term=.b6a46cd79442

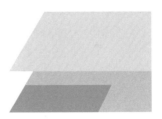

LOVE THIS BOOK?

You can help us share it.
Go to: kevingerald.com/books for a free chapter download to send someone.

Want to buy more books?
Awesome. This book makes a great teaching tool in group settings. We have discounts for group orders. Please contact us at: kevingerald.com/books.

And, don't forget to take the online self-assessment.
Take your free assessment here:

kevingerald.com/books